USE TROUBLE

Other Books by Michael S. Harper

Dear John, Dear Coltrane
History Is Your Own Heartbeat
History As Apple Tree, limited edition
Song: I Want A Witness
Debridement
Nightmare Begins Responsibility
Images of Kin
Healing Song In the Inner Ear
Songlines in a Tesserae Journal, limited edition (with
    Walter Feldman, visuals)
Honorable Amendments
The Family Sequences, limited edition
    (with Walter Feldman, visuals)
Songlines in Michaeltree
Selected Poems [U. K.]
I Do Believe in People, Remembrances
    of W. Warren Harper, 1915-2004
The Fret Cycle, limited edition
    (with Walter Feldman, visuals)
Use Trouble

ANTHOLOGIES
Heartblow, Black Veils
Chant of Saints, with Robert Burns Stepto
Every Shut-Eye Ain't Asleep, with Anthony Walton
The Vintage Book of African American Poetry,
    1750-2000, with Anthony Walton

poems by **MICHAEL S. HARPER**

use T R O U B L E

WITHDRAWN

**UNIVERSITY OF
ILLINOIS PRESS**
Urbana and Chicago

Library of Congress Cataloging-in-Publication Data
Harper, Michael S., 1938–
Use trouble : poems / by Michael S. Harper.
p.   cm.
ISBN 978-0-252-03350-6 (cloth : acid-free paper)
ISBN 978-0-252-07598-8 (pbk. : acid-free paper)
I. Title.
PS3558.A6248U84   2009
811'.54—DC22   2008021824

ACKNOWLEDGMENTS

Some poems appeared in these publications:

American Scholar

Black Scholar

Brilliant Corners

Callaloo

Fourteen Hills

Free Verse

Harvard Review

I Do Believe in People: Remembrances of Walter Warren Harper

Kenyon Review

Kestrel

"NO"

nocturne 3

Notre Dame Quarterly

The Oregon Literary Review

Pembroke

The Best American Poetry 2002

Urbanite

FOR PATRICE CUCHULAIN HARPER

"Bodily decrepitude is wisdom; young
We loved each other and were ignorant."

—"After Long Silence," W. B. Yeats

CONTENTS

III. I Do Believe in People

"For what the writer generally has is not a system of belief but rather AN IMAGINATION of what is radically significant."

—Negative Capability, Nathan A. Scott Jr., p. 129

part **ONE**

THE FRET CYCLE

for Paul Austerlitz

*One takes comfort in the metaphor
reaching for a true image apprehended
in the act of playing.*

FRET (A TUNE NEAR COMPOSITION IN THE STUDIO)

We're just re-tuning among the dials
engineer a student (Chris)   we spoke of Scituate reservoir once

I'm sending him a book in the campus mail
(he has that shorthand   on email   of watery entitlement   a fix)

Paul making new solos in accompaniment writes new music
only he can hear   a praxis of support   near duet, his unction

I watch him 'fret'   over the blur of notched etching awhile back
when we were in the pitch of answering everything behind the beat

we will not be playing today my words now only an arrangement
an order   a pace   but his polishing a notion of fret to hone

what cannot be gone over again in performance   but with dials
amplified in taking away   holding the patterns   for editing

I told him once   (at Madeira's in a list of specials)   anecdotes
of growing up into one's song   he speaks of his father   gone

a stylist of linguistics   from abroad from elsewhere   his mother
less resonant in a solo career   which *hoves* now around tenure   to play

like no other in his sphere   every night   each day   for fresh fret
so we can go back into the zone of talking together over song   riffs

not ever gathered into a garden while he practices new cuisine
hangouts with his sensei   after workouts   to keep his limbered   reed

greased for he seldom orders soup   but fish like ancestry Icelandic
an airline of composition over space   like light near the pole

but his love of warmth   say Dominican Brazil   a talk of equality
in playing amber   smooth   canejuice which can't evaporate at palate

when taste is all vintage of genes like spices in our neighborhood
of an alphabet of notes   declensions   arpeggios   floss   Monk

taking each black key   into embouchures   an attitude   of gloss
vocabulary   a pattern   un-thought out   but felt in fret   his own   soup

'sauce' he says   with olives   the pits a sandpile   reservoir
of studio work   now fret   your folks are waiting   to exit over you

A NOTE FROM CATHY AT YADDO

the dog that bit Patty Sopp   belonged to Katy De Groot
(Fret will occupy her father's house   down by the river

just before studio session)   parable of the bite
for a dog that only guards the premises

Yaddo mascot   no   but De Groots wanted us to know
the story   so play it Paul   on bass clarinet

so the bell   which recites the tones
also catches the pitch of dog

all microphones spiked
in adjacent rooms

THE LESSON FOR PAUL ON CATHERINE CLARKE'S BIRTHDAY

Padre says 'you were bad last night' but not
in performance   wondrous overtones   sonics

to rhyme with tonic and GIN   too much for one
sonata which you could have written   'first thing'

but you were missing breakfast   lunch   De Groot's
ass the apple of your attention   just around the bend

the river where you will compose the suite
of all the ancestors   the factory closed down

after Pearl Harbor   in nearby Whitehall
(remember when you go for your massage

Raymond Moriyasu's   father was in the 442nd in Europe
finally allowed to fight his 'mentors'   in the open

too many Japanese-Americans in Hawaii to encamp
the parachutes we lost in metaphor for easy landings

near fresh water)   you'll play your bass clarinet
fretting for the answers to how to trap the music

not caught in the bell   of Tom Lopez's studio
once a hippie hangout   a lowbrow dream of equity

in another lost cause   you will come to know
the supply line of the Hudson at this crossing stage

of another war (perhaps Page 1 your own) combining
in the nearby fields   a team of mules at the barge

for here was the canal which went to Plattsburgh
an underground rr station for John Brown (Lake Elba)

which is the lesson
as you move your quarters in the woods

FRET IN THE WOODS

Even with drive-up mosquitoes
while you focus on lime

you camp in your head on the river
"ass"   is the feature   heartwork

the slang of ass a full-time job
(praxis a galaxy of women all vintage)

can you stand this ancient proverb
"the song turns into itself as bramble"

somebody got thrown into the briar patch
honeybee and honeystruck pollination

in the next life you will conjure
your own children   the source Bahia

military coups will be native   morpho
(a shirt you own but will not wear

a brand of pollen   attractive   disease
for some species of deceit   caretaker)

the reed is to be listened to   as Coltrane
cautioned   he spent most of his time

conjuring the supreme   right here on
earth   while Elvin was the mask incarnate

country music is what to focus on now
(the bites you get the price: inoculation)

like any cellphone you speak into dark
by calling out tunes you can't remember

when not driving the gig is just ahead
(you fantasize the drive back   easily

don't die on the hwy racing to cabin)
somehow the divine enters your mouthpiece

you will have no more innocence about Y
but you will rewind the clock Fret   less!

TABLE NOTICE

Fret reads this with his lunch
(the day he leaves is when the pool opens

and he takes this personally:
Venezuela, Argentina, Italy, LA

all the muses at the table
he will not swim with them

having left his suit elsewhere)
he takes out his bass clarinet

in the woods where he's been moved
since leaving the 'pink' room

with the pitch machine for jive
upbeats, modulations, adjustments

then he takes the Padre texts
he has recorded and walks that music

into the woods   it is raining   sunny
soon he will be by the river   ax ready

where De Groot might appear to hear
him solo he will be alone that dog

who goes for a walk at the same time
known to bite just anybody if pitch

is tonally correct   and Fret worries
just a little behind the beat   about

this problem   the problem of ass is
very different   juice off the bell

where only partial aspects of sound
can follow   he gives notice   to swim

elsewhere   with Elvin's ghost
which is still hanging around

hung over just a little on gin
ancestral libations having glow

on both sides of the equator
meridian   hemisphere   orisha

preferring fish after he works
tonic with his 'ten' without any tab

I tell him this little initiation
is a trial run   nothing to worry

ass will always be the problem
fascination that does not come only

from Finland his mother's research
at teaching him to read   his father's

linguistic gifts   at being foreign
Fret a true American   loving the music

of every aboriginal birdcall   parse
of organic form his weakness   at

writing it all down   then explication
to tame the critics   while he hears ass

apologizes for it   the stiff drink juice
across his lap   while waiting to enter

this part of the ensemble   improvised
players coming and going   some who read

others who can't and won't   compress
that part of the schedule   Fret won't

ever be the same   he knows this truth
he ponders the fact of the river   dog

pitch   ass   mother who made him study
prepare   father who outlived her

didn't do right by her   or so he thinks plays the
aria of Yaddo (meaning shadow)

FRET SKIPS TOWN FOR A GIG IN NEW LONDON

Recording machine goes with him
though he says otherwise; lost sessions

bother him ass does not   he speculates
what's catchable is like gin   disappearing

guaranteeing nothing in the creative tank
(yet he struggles with routes   only)

his fetish is to play badly for money
(he thinks I don't see this obsession

but Yaddo allows failure every day   studio
in the woods also   East Room no picnic)

he misses the witticisms of bacon and cakes
(not the Bruce variety but french toast

the inmates love it   syrup like molasses
which I attribute to rum trade cane flax)

We will take this up when Haiti swims up
the many bodies of the deep in his craw

We will get some Finland stories   Nokia
fishkill   serfs   pogroms   lute fantasies

an instrument akin to ass   he says   sleep
walking his way to the lotion to dose

Pulitzer's new rules   where he can stand up
make changes   run down Lacy   who just died

I must point out the change of name in obit
Astaire not able to dance any rhythm

but no slouch with partners   film   silent
it doesn't matter   ugly   nice threads

FRET DEEP IN THE WOODS

Untuned piano still the birds flock
your sessions prodigious (Elvin   spirit

now is lone accompaniment he had no
children in "Nagasaki" or "Pontiac"

but the pied piper of drums calls
you can't help but answer)   behind wheel

tunes collapse around your ears
(the smell of women   torment you)

you play into and over them for praxis
they write their names on your feet

you begin to clean up around the flat
(little mini-recorder punishments   regal)

you stop drinking entirely   meals fallow
toasts in the town are unfriendly   muse

talks into the meadow across the night
(you can hear horses   winnowing silence

across the lap of your shoes   anklets
silk shirts   the gift of the morpho

alive at riverside)   libation   libation
in every element   you try to go home

early but the melodies have you gutshot
you learn to walk with such pain   soldier

formations   bayonets   infantry lore
sonnets file onto the memo stand   padre

has told you so   you will listen   faintly
put aside the staggered machine: orchestrate

FRET LEAVES YADDO

Because you are drinking beer
the missing of breakfast is strategy

some leave notes others want you
to drop by   but packing is proverbial

and not to be tested   like water
in the dirty swimming pool

where you can wash your clothes
while you 'chat' en route to email

some you'll meet in new york
others will compress your shuttle

into the weave of materials
the craft of   'making' modest but steady

nest is the order of the day
(last night you saw a deer robust

the leaping factor bright
like the eyes of the hunted

Fret thinks of Haitian music
the cost of that music   artmaking

with or without the military)
G8 goes on in Sea Islands   Gipper

gives the nation a holiday   called
'the communicator'   lest you forget

you have been doing in your studio
East Room is not pink room

the pitch moves   the tent is collapsed
Vermont two hours north   paydirt

GHOST OF FRET AT HIGH TABLE: MANSION

Bouquet squats at center   peonies
Chinese garden music Fret   quips

sits on the lap of the redhead   forlorn
Fiona's papa squeezes all juice

from the Philharmonic   vegetarian   mama
Juilliard stuck tightens the hold   pox

americana   jogger killed   for no reason
not far from the bridge   Fret plays

for the young and old asses of the apple
but does not get lost on city politics

he slyly puts the touch on redhead
(Padre told him about that melody

just one note   one finger   on sweet spot)
he moves to the silent table   a patch

but one of fresh soil   Blows his ax
one last time   his cellphone on quiet

so allcanhear   his solo   Music Room
ready   acoustics   like cathedral tones

at Dutch's flagdraped caissondrug coffin
(Vermont's homebrew faint now   riffs

he could not learn in school now evident
in all his muscles   the soft reed   broken)

but 'strong in the broken places'   chants
slowly into the vacant seat beside him

the ghost—ancestor analogy touches
the master chords   he memorizes

FRET'S NEWS FROM THE FRONT: YADDO AFTER

Provost with no pouilly-fuisse power
to bring back Ray Charles "Robinson"

sends a word in channels   protest
prairie dogs put up resistance

redhead pigeontoed painter   no dreds
keeps prancing around   the premises

lost   but steady   martini glasses   still
in the back fridge   Katy   always   on

expenses   has left the building   'hello'
more resonant than...   "goodbye"

I noticed Daniel pour repaired convertible
with a local washing   off to   New

Hampshire on personal maneuvers   found
several clumps of   honeybees   in tower

but   like the snapping turtle   keeping
his distance   cellphone   opera   localfair

on the ready   Fiona read about her father
in the nyt   his 'animal'   implements

a swimming pool   opening outdoors   from
inside   her psychiatric meanderings   no

longer disguised   in treatments   Phil-
harmonic   Mr. caisson is gone   dimes

still belong to FDR   Nancy   chastened
on her knees at sunset   (you don't have

any Irish brogue I can fathom   so get
yourself   a   'Jewish' lawyer)   and sue   bad

MARTINI GLASSES GALORE

Ten and Russian gone but vermouth
a trace no olives bandits ate 'em

around the perennial fire of night
the makers gather   lying   prostrate

in their rooms   bats occasionally
enter chased down by nets   upside

down a yoga expert turns back nyc
upsidesmanship   murder   mayhem breach

in town the stablefiretenders come
north   cats   calming the horses

I see them at the Yaddo lakes   fishing
or watching the undertow of branches

take the silt   minnows   bass   survive
barely under the trees   the woods gut

spin out the filters of dust   mariners
come in SUVs   to garden the roses

by standing guard   occasional marriages
at the rose garden   oldtimers search

for the magical goldfish   long gone
actuarial tables stand up in clearings

a girl dances with her father   brother
can hardly walk for the shoes   staggers

away from childhood into children   bold
for not paying attention to her mother

but who listens glow of part time ease
steady work of making due   do or don't

FRET SHOWS UP AT THE METROPOLITAN

She's leaving town for the apple   to sell
her wares on paper   contacts made on this

coast need phyla on that   agents galleries
gone sour   such delicate Mondrian corsets

spread out in precision   girdles back in
place   her stopping her work for four years

to recover   start again   a world missing
chastitybelt now an iron cage at exhibit

fitted into place   cameras she bought
unworkable   target   cvs failing except

for you   your instrument in your hands
the best part of her on paper   her heart

pounding as she packs up leaving wine
for Padre   who's written a short madrigal

in her honor   asked back in this detail
the stay in Albany no blue hwy in leather

you break training for a day and let her
in an inch   the neckline broken   lost

weight   an appetite for all but food
lunches wasted   the steak she orders

in her head the first meal when apple
turns to core   heart   and brain show up

together   you intuit all   this with gigs
you should turn down   but drawn near her

you find the Met your mother did research
in remember   she left space for this paper

THE LIST: YADDO

You will not be in touch with her
who has given up her wine   unopened

Argentina   California   an hour in
from the vineyards   Mondrian's

artform sessions of composition
do not hide tears of the heart

ruthless in colorational design
medicines bought on camera infect

you said nothing late into evening
when I swim into your caverns   whist

a strategy of containment   bidwar
you cannot fathom by touch alone

the train you take N or S   empty
but collectible   caboose an axial

table where the dining is exquisite
to the tongue   but to the eye   illusory

the flesh goes bad over the trestles
we are saying goodbye in code   emails

handwritten only in another century
bionosphere   newsreels   documentaries

the still frame is best   negatives
large enough to contain   our world

our children though we have none
collect   admire   admonish   eviscerate

backwards   in stereo   typescript
illegible   the soul leaves the body

FRET LEAVES YADDO IN DISGUISE

Her perfume arrests   she gives Padre
two bottles of wine   Argentina red

California white the desert within her
only an hour east of San Francisco

but bleak   she will not speak before noon
(again the papers   her paper   Mondrian

another gallery   another museum run   back
east   trainride all alone to the apple

blessing)   she will eat a large steak
and lavish the cooking for herself   mirror

touched up hair   she should not speak
to him by cell   payphones are delicious

when you're hungry   losing weight   blind-
sided by passions   long adrift   when she

stopped   working her designs   surrounded
by vegetarians   the fish   run   away from

her scaling knife   wriggling on drawing
board   dorsal fin   potent squid   be still

he would have driven her to her city
but his trunk is far too small   baggage

of this quality   demanding attention
he can not give   obsessive Argentinean

Venezuelan   Italian ass   now fading
into the red fleece above his lap

the one melody she teaches on his tongue
requiring new fingering   fresh reeds

FRET HAVING SURVIVED MODERNITY

The ax falls in the meadow   Goliath
turns the sling has but one rock

but it is the rock of ages   Fret
listens to the painters of old   musicians

will fail him if he's not steady
(alive on the table of redsweetened hair

he can do no evil and no good   just stand)
this will be a fight to the finish

as legend attests   instrumentation capsizes
but the solo melodic note rises toward him

the giant who's been foreshadowed by fall
and lost an eye in the process   retreats

the lawyers come into the picture   Fret
likes his chances   he cares not for battle

but resumé   long lists of charts   headcase
that he is standup only when he has to

he marvels at speed in practice   mornings
(late at night   fantasies   extraordinary

while playing *live*)   with makeshift   ovoid
players   tambourines   choirs   caped maestros

for he is all things at once   symphonic
the piano answers the strings   oboes nod

he prefers homemade melodies   folksay
but damsel gives him purpose   he strides

across all crevices   all declensions
rabbi turns away from all texts   passover

he prefers holyrollers in makeshift haunts
(he builds in the basement of structures

beneath thresholds he's known before death)
annunciations that circle of glow triumphs

  [he becomes prime   prostrates himself
A   E   I   O   U]

FRET DISCOVERS THE BLUES, AGAIN

He got the thought   twice she was
ambidextrous   it was not her art

but her stride   pigeontoed   losing weight
with each step   chortling speech   at her

own juice   which were prodigious
having lost her gallery   stopped working

on paper   for four years   married again
the pink of her eyes framed in sterile

blue   which made the orbs   enchanting
when she closed her lids   then opened

everything to hold him close   to kill
his fear   his attitude   his pledge

not to fall into orbs   the Finnish
especially when displaced   became linguist

saturated   drank   too much   or not at all
and turned   technological   even when

fishing in shallow water   the deep   so
transporting by reflection   were classic

Norse highlights sprung into song   lore
eyeshadow taught him what blacks   down

South   brought with them on trains   buses
knapsacks   shopping bags   chickenhawk

songs of cottontail and rabbit   briarpatch
the light and the dark transmogrified

He'd fall for this woman's touch   forgot
himself   wrote melodies to her reflection

ASS

She pops holding him in place   refusing
to scratch any part of him   yet holding

him in place   a pouch   hamstrings opening
wetness prodigious   he cannot talk about

any of this but plays his ax   recklessly
a suite selects itself in the bathing

juices from the unopened vaults   reckoning
the pain gone   fleece of locks   prisons

keys   a burst of hormones he cannot name
refusing to speak in the middle of lavish

kisses   the french know nothing when it
comes   to this bragging   talking shit

as though what stinks doesn't inflame
the body   into the mind   of no comparison

he washes his laundry   but not her sheet
the standing pole   where she whispers

his name   a text spoken for the first time
the food for thought   in appetite   spices

condiments without an ounce of fat on it
'he means you' the sediment of solos stolen

he begins to study the discipline of quality
he thought he could count in practice

the body swells and closes down   he rests
but when she's near   he puts his fingers

in the openings   what musicians call 'breaks'
the looking around for options   new moves

letting her lead   forgetting to hold back
(he straddles the extreme unction of coitus

delivered and held back) stud that you are
this is the perfume you live for   seldom get

FRET IN STUDIO WITH THE ANCESTORS

Without libation but in spirit   makeshift camera
he makes devotions *á la condomblé*

then popping his finger   asks for playback
"twiddlin' thumbs"   the metaphors for passing over

the dark passages of the soul we conjure in Tom
Lopez's country studio   right on the Hudson River at riverside

Fret has been practicing his own music scaring him with inventions
bass clarinet talking to him   free of microphones

the De Groot summer home in tune to riffs
he seldom imagines at eventide   sunset

looking west over every canebreak
he stomps   finger popping   off tempo

he's swum   in the pond   to refresh
eaten lunch   fidgets   as is his proxy   to finishing

melodies   awaken the craw   'magic circle'   he breathes
in circularity   another lesson   outta school

as he hands me Brother "RAY"   in heaven
DVD   the world of jetlag descends

booty palms for booty lessons   of the flesh   and spirit
a baker's dozen of Fret   lessons   building

toward a saga   under the surface   rivers
make you sing   when out of the woods

oxygen   one more element
to swim   by meridians   steady

FRET FINDS THE INSTRUMENT OF ARCHIPELAGO

She would be Chinese because of the spices
he gets this rush when watching the diving

needs no olympics   yet his mind wanders over the framing
of points level of difficulty   entry into the water

he admits to liking the wet hairs of the point system
when he sees the pool thinks of the rivers that need crossing

that which is ancient that which is new   collect as attitude
a passion for rum of the best vintage for his birthday

well, he takes into his arms the tenor soprano   his fingering intricate
as she said when he had her up against the walls of perspiration

we can't call it sweat because his attention span in studio
is nothing like the bandstand   yet Fret comes alive at audio

the mask is the dance of adumbration
he is at home in that nation thinks maroon runaway   creation

MT. PLEASANT LOCAL LIBRARY

Van is there from Barrington
Nancy Craven without the shakes

Fret ready to blow (Emily cool with baritone
maneuvers   from Seattle footwork he can't see

for she escaped the bombs in Madrid trainsense
a long diary of muslims with issues)

I sit down while Fret stands up librarians
in kidchairs all about I start off with

"The Myth of Music" to steady my beat
for all the kids in the audience and one

turns to her father and says "I love you
Dad" right on time and in key about eight

The rest is routine   except Fret is too close
attention-span vexed (he wants to solo)

then Emily comes in   terse poignant "Harris
Collection" ready   with Dickinson embers

just above the transom for the parents
who are glad they came to the children's

section of the neighborhood all poems come
from there my daughter's riffs "Nasty Poet"

building a literate way new avenue her own
house petition to dreams only she can make

FRET FINDS THE OPEN FIELD

I have told Fret about my former teacher Henri Coulette who wrote a poem
on the subject "Tenure"   it is buried in his COLLECTED POEMS   long
    out of print

the picaro comes to mind because all the masters tell long stories
Sterling Brown would say   "they're trying to bury the hatchet,

and it's always in my head"   and Count called Tatum's felicities on piano
"the Hatchet"   looking for a job in Pittsburgh   asking for favors 'from the
    help'

before the master came in   and he always arrived early   for practice
(minimalism was always the approach to Basie's band after that lesson)

I will not announce Move or 'The Tulsa Riot' of 1921 when the black section
was bombed from above   in the first instance of civilian blitzkrieg

(lessons learned by trench warfare during World War I)
I noticed you doctored the order of the compositions   crafted hot off the
    press

in your name you took what you wanted   left the rest   for other picaros
(I told you about my 'epic of search' in the stacks of the l.a. state open stacks

the early coursework from insiders who migrated as birds toward paradise)
BIRD was the first that got my attention   see my poem on BEAN in
    HONORABLE AMENDMENTS

on Waterloo and mud   we both know you would be hell if only six feet tall
the instrument you've selected to depart the field of play on the Pembroke
    campus

contrabass clarinet silver in appearance a hum of switches at your feet for
    effect
"Ilu: The Talking Drum" by Etheridge   Knight   conman   prisoner   addict
    prince

starts the program   Obeng a head full of proverbs   on all his African
    percussion
cunning company to Royal's drumming   roommate   soulsinger   stand-in
    for Elvin

we poured libation for him from the balcony of Yaddo's mansion above
 kitchen
in this kitchen of the campus we pour mountain dew cachaça canejuice conjo

lost in performance the self lets the cork out of the bottle   wafts over
 audience
benign or malign   your enemies will be
 transformed   audio   video   condomblé

the religion of the elders   in both worlds   comes forward ancestor worship
(man as artform   women   as singers   children   the fresh space of our
 waters)

WORD DRUM   DRUM WORD might be the answer to ancestry
lest we forget our beings/becomings are to thrive in the world of living   true

'a light is asked for and a light is given' 'simply human is what their faces say'
I know today's lesson   the making of the possible now cipherable   fretsome
 cryhue

part **T W O**

You told this to the children
when they confessed their works

were incomplete

A PHOTOGRAPHIC GUIDE TO THE CITY

Your probings take me back
to old neighborhoods:
Ivy Street
a gay alley
when gay meant other:
the fireman, his ax
held high,
being shown the door
to the fire
standing open,
the plants
in the yard
fireproof
the gaslite
of the fireplace
a visage
of her mother
as a child
having just given up
a child.
I stood on Miramar
without a gate
to protect me
and paid my Mexican
landlord
reasonable rent
for a house
with a backyard
my first son
could play in:
all the houses
were pastel;

driving through the fog
to Junipero Serra
WOMAN IN LOVE
seminar
and tutorial
where she learned
what she could not
learn at home:
the teacher as sentry.

Your brother
(with Francisco
half Peruvian
half German)
in fresh lederhosen
rode his scooter
down to the trolleyline
at Ocean Avenue
just for the fun of it,
avoiding the tracks
effortlessly
at the last moment.

Every day
with eucalyptus
on his fingers
he sucked
his Swenson's
ice cream cone
gasping
at Alcatraz
and the cable car
line,
majesty
of the Stern Grove
swing

in his homemade
sweater.

And he loved the zoo.

We were at the beach,
waiting for his mother's
class to end,
when a boy
all of thirteen
ran into the sea
of lsd
and washed up
two days later
at Seal beach.

This is the beginning
of homicide
as a father
knows it,
his woman
in another man's arms
and legs;
here is where one
no longer loves
the city
where your firstborn
struggled
to breathe
in the isolette
while his mother
kept her milk
coming
with a pump.

Then: regret
at not being friendly

with Stanford
medical research
on hyaline membrane,
so your sons died:
and your mother
did not cry.

This is the hormone
you carry:
this guide to the city.

USE TROUBLE

for Jacob Armstead Lawrence
1917–2000, in memoriam

You told this to the children
when they confessed their works

were incomplete   your dignity   grace
a mapped space   for trouble

your *migration* series   at   23
synaptic code for having nothing

as you built off the backs of the poor
your symmetries where paint was talk

"gumbo yaya"   Hayden   (your collaborator)
coined it about his native paradise valley

a nourishment of the Detroit ghetto
while you were content with Harlem

a sixty-block walk to MoMA
for filial instruction

of the Italian Renaissance:
now in Seattle they lay you down

those parts Indian of your heritage
in Chief Seattle's words:

"This we know—
All things are connected   like the blood"

migraines at gunpoint
bullet-ridden   love song   as migrants

to the highest plane
a vast battlefield of tones

over vegetation of the visible
where there is no insurance

yet   in retrospective   fantasy
to remake the spirit in your name

PORTRAIT: (JAY SAUNDERS REDDING AT SAYLES HALL) 5/26/97

*"That night as I lay in bed in the little town of Gabriel, a
thousand miles from all that had meant refuge, I felt at home
and at peace, even with all that lay ahead of unending struggle
(for I was not blind to this) and remaking in the faintly
glimmering future. This was victory for me, not triumph.
No man alone can ever know such triumph as
I had hope for in the years ahead."*

—*No Day of Triumph*

Portrait from a photograph;
the robe svelte as Ajax

dignity no overseer could touch;
when he wrote legions were his follicle

the notion of democracy
so deep his pleats contused

at any denial
of the individual

hard times after the year 2000
easy times in the hall

where you can sit,
listening to the grand organ

and find your way
in seminars of the sacred

your protection of the country
as you knew it

willed to be known;
love yourself first

so you can love the world
losing your chattel

in architecture
build a great house

in the wilderness
unuttered inside

the prosody of becoming;
style is your era

and you should implant it
as signature to your whirl:

learn to dance the Lindy hop
(remember silhouettes

that you have been
as you aged near the wall

and leaping over it
at vespers, at epiphany

gave everything back
in the great getting-up in the morning)

this is a day of triumph for you:
this is the frame.

ESTHER

No telling what zone of healing
you need to enter after Jean Toomer's death

portrait: I have done a few for your husband,
Jay Saunders Redding, and call his natal day,

and erase your sanguine commentary
about shortness of breath

your ears and eyes failing,
your hopes to get to your 93rd birthday

2 21 00 your clarity commands
as your two sons do their father's bidding

from the far side of Toomer's resonance
on beauty and violation,

your husband's NO DAY OF TRIUMPH,
his portrait in Sayles Hall now quatrains

from my wary students on assignment
about how democracy, race, and stylistics

are their own portrait gallery:
how slavery is never over in these Americas

so much of what is lost cumulative
in a gloss that few record

as you dream of another life
standing under the Emancipation Tree   on Hampton's campus.

Saunders is about to assist in Washington
at the National Endowment for the Humanities

then to abide at another ivy league outpost
when all he wants to do is write

the pleasures of composition
he would get up early for

and at the end
cannot write his name

I relish telling you this
in mock couplets of invention

I was made to carry
at my grandma's knee

portraits of the ancestors
posing as relatives

relatives
alive as ancestors

TRIUMPHS

for Jay Saunders Redding

*"That night as I lay in bed in the little town of Gabriel, a
thousand miles from all that had meant refuge, I felt at home
and at peace, even with all that lay ahead of unending struggle
(for I was not blind to this) and remaking in the faintly
glimmering future. This was victory for me, not triumph.
No man alone can ever know such triumph as I had hope
for in the years ahead."*
—No Day of Triumph

Hands that still shake
with indignation;
around the family tree
the Delaware Indians;
on the high ground
the Civil War distracts
the fast water:
in this dream running up-hill—
is the dream of the document—
it is written in both hands.

Odd moments in the classroom,
odder moments at board meetings,
the arcane secrets with only this memo
of the ancestors,
your plaque of sacred names
seen at first light,
the light of your mother's room
where there is frost, and the frost's glow.

The high color of this season,
the parceling of books
you could never touch again,

perhaps these mulch
in the John Hay Library,
in your elegant prose,
and the poem's doodle
on the nation's brain.

Trustees of the college,
the deadlight of the swamp,
owls swift as the interstate,
Esther packing your Arrow shirts
for the nation's capitol,
and abroad the *Ramayana*,
and Sanskrit tablets,
the good discipline of service,
your sons like envelopes of octane
on a winding hill.

Conservative, in the quiet pines,
in the little good soil
not broken away;
Liberal as the sage,
picked up in the valley
in drifts of change,
hopes of permanent change,
which is tradition,
which is community
where we try to live;
which is literacy,
the hallowed face of the deed.

On your birthday, 80 years old
on good days, as your face is not,
though it is a strong face,
when looked into, then
looking away, the structures
of a life are framed:
patriot, craftsman, dome.

HOMAGE TO JAY SAUNDERS REDDING
ON HIS NATAL DAY: 10 13 04

You would be ninety-nine or so the lines in *Auden's*
famous poem 'of modern life' he refused to stop revising

I read you *NO DAY OF TRIUMPH* nowadays
scan your portrait in Sayles Hall (stolen from a *photograph*

that John Forasté never lets me forget at earlybird swim)
like every poet of the image he has lost his job

but found his vocation in archetypal recovery of the *turn*
I read you Hayden's *"October"* on your porch   in *Ithaca*

Esther holding court the belle of the local order of saints
above and below ground her sons monitoring the last days

while the first belong to you Wilmington   Delaware
proud beyond the warfare of the local Indians neighbor

of Clifford Brown's people Brownie the best horn player
of his generation   and sound on the piano

gave Miles his due in Detroit when Miles was strung out
(then went home to his father's farm in Illinois to clean up)

miscellany of the call to board of fellow service
handwritten note from Howard Swearer thanking me for *"Ajax"*

whom you resemble in your stance on race democracy 'the word'
the girl who gave a certain order to your papers in the archives

is buying flowers for you both on this your Keatsian holiday
"To Autumn" though in California Pasadena no less where your son

is not fully retired from the missiles of the age
we lunched at Huntington where my teacher *Christopher Isherwood*

taught me nothing I could use except the pallor of the lost souls
between the wars never mentioned his father who died in World War I

sent me off to face the draft board in *Des Moines* to drop my trousers
to a medical student from *Waterloo* where black strikebreakers stayed pat

I saved the tintype of 'the padre' for a memorial booklet in remembrance
of my father and spliced two missives as portraiture of your visage

honorand par excellence role model benefactor spy in the enemies ward
passive-aggressive mentor to *Gandhigy* handwritten blotto *'brother'*

the lawyer who fought against gerrymandering before the fashion
of being photographed 'at large' in tempo *out of tempo*

the slow tempo of prose you wrestled into form when lesser men and women
turned to getting even at **Penn** against all odds you sat out

several black aesthetics rounds of play with superiors one *Nobel*
counted your lessons 'in the canebrake' found humor in the dunciad

of Sterling's quip about the black fraternity house you never settled in
gourmets is what prof. called them *thoroughgood* the best of dirty jokesters

I tell you this just before your centennial before apotheosis
where *'memories are old identities'* and "**how to read**" your text

PRAISESONG FOR BB

In the movie "The Postman" Pablo Neruda
is in exile on an island in Italy
(unable to go home)

the postman delivers his mail
the only literate customer
(on a bicycle)

soon a woman appears as bartender
Beatrice of the plantains you might conjure
(also Dante's "Beatrice")

we know from the cut of the film
there is a tragedy, and a child
(little Pablito)

the postman dies at a demonstration
which is only the reading of the one poem
(who can be a communist in a film)

the essence of your film is on the cutting room floor
but it might be a dance floor: Apollo, Howard, Savoy
(tunes in the upper registers)

lindyhopping is permissible
'swinging those chicks in reefer glow
(Count Basie's band is blowing)

for each spirit over furlongs, every pitstop
the regimen of the hours is in the sky
(hawk is your favorite bird of paradise)

we have known plantations and Palmares runaways
and ease into maroon conditions
(on maneuvers in flight, in mud, in Butler)

with the commissary at an open fire
Rosewood, Leonard Wood, Pimloco
(basic training is just fundamentals)

the corps does not allow women to make men
so image, uniform, tact, kindness
(sweat in workouts make for stellar games)

conditioning the prance of the cooldown
flareups predictable and expected
(shower of effects, pinot noir)

Douglass might have been born on this day
he saw his mother seldom, grandma more
(the beard the talisman of manhood)

walked five miles to work and back
from Cedar Hill to Anacostia
(boarded up his wife's room at death)

three autobiographies his anthems to change
literacy giving measure to caulking ships
(have you written your memoirs?)

schemata of cost control at Nashville
the rainbow faces alive in research
(singing at Jubilee Hall at Fisk before the choir)

so you have earned your day at parade rest
obstacle courses remain, in temperance
(as we consider the view from elsewhere)

the sacred names will not be latitude
in this proem, unutterable as the sacred
(and you must conjure them and complete reveille)

fly with the wind, hawkeye,
descend from canopy to the understory
(tell the story in increments)

we will share (again) the primal anecdotes
that only warriors hear in Monk's harmonies
(heard melodies sweet, unheard sweeter)

to take 2000 as porkchop hill
and change the parallels to longitude
(watching the whales in Pip's company)

GOODBYE TO ALL THAT

---

for Bernard E. Bruce, Sr.

Keep in mind the timetable
of goodbyes, titanic, microscopic

a nuanced story of what is withheld
in close company, what revealed

thank you for letter re Gayl Jones
to the Howard Foundation

handwriting on the wall is punchline
for shrinks, eggheads, lover of mussels

stairman before there was such a machine
diagnostician, winecellar connoisseur

master of couchtherapy, cockpit cellphone
customer service, off-minor memos

a handwriting dry as the Sahara
at home in Papua New Guinea

with tales of Farrakhan's violin
and his mentor, Malcolm X, alive on tape

I will remind you Michael Brennan
was the local Irish mafia on campus

as economist, who told the Harper/Jones
consultancy there was no pool

and no candidates, but agreed to send
the job description to augment, to prune

no beards thick enough, no pate shiny enough
no better keys to the elevator

no better decoder of desegregation orders
those orders never taken as educational

except in reminders on the internet
at Arlington, in the soup of praxis

in stadium runways, Olympic Trials,
Providence Plantation still requiring

written passes in the hand of Frederick Douglass
who broke the gate of the White House

to give his spoken opinion
of Lincoln's Second Inaugural

and which I recall now as words of honor and pledge
to your antics in protection of us

Fred Douglass said to A. Lincoln
"it was a sacred effort."

So we will track this on video in closequarters
with vintage wine, zoom lenses, stereo vistavision

as remembrance of our present trials:
repeat after me: "it was a sacred effort."

PUBLIC LETTER: VISIBLE INK

in memory of Howard R. Swearer (1932–1991)

By a "commitment to democracy" I mean a commitment
to the idea that there are no fixed or determinable limits to
the capacities of any individual human being, and that all
are entitled, by inalienable right, to equal opportunities to
develop their potentialities. Democracy in this sense is an
ideal, not a political system, and certainly not an actual state
of affairs.

— *"The Beer Can by the Highway"* by John A. Kouwenhoven

I.

You were at your best,
at the airport,
in brief convergings,
half in the dark,
in tourist class,
after windsprints,
the high hurdles just taken:
always the Wichita Indians
in the townsquare,
handwriting on the walls,
and in the fields,
chaff
"amber waves of grain."

Chaff was for direction,
for clarity and purpose:
"Across Kansas:"
"My state still dark,
my dream too long to tell."

You stick in the public good,
for which you were a stick in the mud,

your handwritten notes
quite discernible,
approaching pidgin.
For the public park
we will select Toad Island,
inviting the wasted beer can
as reflector,
to the errant estate,
where you could play
the pottery of vernacular
into its proper idiom,
utensils,
with tensile strength.

Lie down on the infamous Arkansas river,
which is an attitude of promise,
serpentine, chaotic, overflowing
in drought where overruns flourished:
we will touch the kiln
of geography, moving westward
as dawn does
to all lions on the path.

II.

This is the part of the joke,
the parenthetical, the process
which is the American vernacular:
it is more than speech; it partakes
of action, on the grid, the alloy
of it a skin called aeromechanics,
though it is anything but mechanical:

The Joke   (A 100K employer says to a job-
seeker, "I will give you a job;
sweep out the store;" "but I'm a Brown
graduate, the old he/she protests:
OK comes a wimpish reply, "I'll show you how.")

Peace is our own abundance
offered to others as self-creation,
so you stand for the public good;

but you do more: the harmony
of mutual frustration
haunts the campus:
your own speculations
tend toward skyscrapers
because there is great will
in the prairies, couplings
of trains and bridges
with great space all around;
the country's intellect
sits more comfortably
in colonial mansions:
you will never feel at home;
still, a book of Mark Twain's
sayings helps on the trail
as you build toward the stadium:
"American houses with Queen Anne fronts
had Mary Ann behinds."

From Russia, as you wait for your bags,
you think of their absence of phonebooks:
new amalgams of thought, of emotion,
spread as an attitude, but how do you find
people at the confluence of rivers,
seat of Sedgwick county,
trading post, sprocketing
into Chisholm Trail, railroad
center, oil refinery,
aircraft engineering,

meat packing; how do you sprocket
the good life for meateaters.

On the Pacific,
eucalyptus trees,
die of the cold; park rangers
leave them as ghosts
dancing on the perimeter
on gorgeous hills, the Santa Ana
winds
in the wrong direction
spread those trees like wildfire
as they burst in the heat
of windtunnels in the bad compass.

The country is frozen in Rorschach
tests with no inkling
of where to find the inky cap,
the mushroom on the inkwell,
an oilwell refined into energy
that does fit as fertilized goose eggs.

"We must improve on the odds
of fifty poor melons to produce
one good one;" we must improve ourselves
with abundance.

III.

Students parade into the Rockefeller
Library, past the portrait of Inman Page,
class orator, runagatebenefactor
of the talented tenth: we are back
on paper in the library,
amnesty and amendments
in the framed oil portrait
of an orator, who writes,
for the word is flesh,
and some flesh is political
as the Civil War was political

on paper, cantilevers over
empty space so you could perch
behind the cutting bar
and see what is cutting;
this playfulness
will customize in the eye
and our taste in other fields.

We will not forget the short
net, and the doublefaults
of making idle conversation.

We must model the iguana;
for court appearances
the cape is best,
at firestations,
all people are children
of the supreme being,
no one is a child of the earth.

A few fingers on the celestial bowl
is for governance; we will serve
before and after we go to school.

All smokescreens are a walk in woods
on holdovers, past and future;
one must get one's hands
on the garden and one's own tools
out of these simple pleasures,
complex fate.

The pond (from the air) is a river
of spider webs, of sunflowers;
such simple loveliness,
all things alive,
have their constant tension.

A toast for your stiff upper lip;
all that cascades from its amphora.

DUBONNET

in memory of Ewart Guinier

You said you wanted me to sign on
for three years   sentence on the Harvard contract

you will be paid equal to your stature
since there is   no possibility of tenure here

do not expect any white students
Eliot and the other houses will not permit

though you may use the library
no   guarantee of parking privileges

but I always pay for lunch
and you may drink whatever if you're not teaching

Du Bois was almost a friend of mine
he was at Iowa long before you   married a hawkeye

lived to regret it   the nesting of radicals
in either sex   an ordeal particularly when gathering

research (he could not mean Sam Hose
who was so accurate with an ax he killed a plantation

owner with one stroke of his anvil
Du Bois stopped walking downtown to meet Joel Chandler

Harris when he saw Sam's fingers and toes
in the local meatmarket

he was truly too genteel to mention any of this
immaculate as a haberdashery before Harvard Square

was square:) sign this   he said
feel free to go to faculty meetings   you teach on Fridays

traffic will teach you a lesson
your reputation precedes you   therefore   summer stipend

I will be on MV if you need me
but you won't need me

remember the strategies of the islands
cricket and no cricket   and sugar mills

why I drink Dubonnet   to remind me of French
manners on the breath of Napoleon   again from an island

You must share an office take mine
my daughter and her mother have me every Friday

teach as though you belong on the Advocate
remember Du Bois didn't think much of the Renaissance

though he loved Harlem
hated hanging the lynchingbee flag out naacp headquarters

———————

ARCHIVES: THE PUBLIC LIBRARY I

———————

in memory of RALPH WALDO ELLISON, 1914–1994

"But great artists never imitate their equals;
* they plagiarize from their inferiors."*
—André Malraux

One was named for you
in the town you were born,
almost everything finetuned
into music, dance music:
any kid knows most streets

are meant to destroy him;
and women die on the branch.

And birds sing: nightingales,
crows, tanengers, owls,
aspects of the human
nomenclature of the divine
as ninety-nine sacred names
on the seams of your brow
and you a child of slavery
with ministers of each spectrum
transforming the flocks
as on "Juneteenth,"
when word finally reached
Galveston, Texas
that the war was over
and every soul had to employ
be productive,
feed himself, feed others,
and refuse to eat
of his brother, his sister,
no matter the hue & cry,
no matter miscegenation

that city is on no hill
you can fathom
outside the family
you have made
and denied
so we will commence
with the cemetery
where the flowers
are nameable as peace
abundant as prairie
every Indian a clan
each clan a language

whose edibles
cannot be written down
and remembered
ritual being the mother
of unbearable pressure
and what to comprehend
as the earth cannot be
owned but maneuvered
in spiritual claim
for a perfected process:
density of detritus,
bones, amulets, rituals
of invention
as one survives
nothing but what is
beyond us: the use of us
a beneficence
after weaponry
after unhusbanded
improvisation
against one's fears
and every woman
shaman for technologists
nuclear children
in the nuclei
a polyglot
escrescence
improvenander
boomerang
facefulness
sipped modally
from needful air
from cold fire
pure voicefulness
no trained incapacity

here, thus
antagonistic cooperation
in the pentad
made triangular
slave trader
in the quadrants
of the heavens
which is self-invention
self-promotional glee
at what no one
could have made
before the process

and that process changed
utterly, utterly changed
in the living
which is deathless
dying: dying's
not death, do not grieve
as you wash away
unnerving tears
in ceaseless voyaging
in cities
in prairies
deep within
in aboriginal calm
an original blessing

ARCHIVES: THE PUBLIC LIBRARY II

A Poetic Address to the Minerva Awards Recipients, NYPL, NYC

> *"Believe me, I loved you all.*
> *Believe me, I knew you, though faintly, and I loved, I*
> *loved you*
> All."
> —Gwendolyn Brooks from her poem, THE MOTHER

Today is Gwendolyn Brooks's birthday.
She raised enough hell as one of three
judges for a contest, which I did not win,
and DEAR JOHN, DEAR COLTRANE was published:
it was rejected, often; its original title,
BLACK SPRING in conflict with a book
written and published by Henry Miller:
mine was a very different book:
I gave up that title; one university press
told me, to my face, they already had one
black book of poetry for their list:
then our Miss Brooks came along.
In her letter to me, a beginner whom she did not know,
she wrote: YOU WERE MY CLEAR WINNER!

As you know Minerva is really Athena,
helpmate of Odysseus in need,
full of brainpower and regal assignation:
you have permission to write, as Minerva
designates, a letter, sent registered mail,
with my return address: you were my clear winner:

Minerva valedictorians
of our five boroughs
are pentagons,
Kenneth Burke's theory

of the pentad is symbolic dramaturgy,
a democratic theory of action
on the human stage of your world:
make it yours by making yourself
in a framed adaptation
of your expectations:
it was Burke who analyzed the malign
cadences of Hitler's speeches;

it is a difficult book to keep in print,
but it is 'equipment for living'

as our Miss Brooks, master storyteller,
reminds us about our losses:

I don't know why my mother wants to stay here,
this old world ain't been no friend to her:

my mother taught me to read
before I went to PS 25
during World War II,
before I went to school;
her mother would moan,
while ironing, and listening
to the soaps: sometimes, I feel,
like a motherless
child; I heard her because I had
skipped school, ridden the subway
to Van Courtland Park,
or Carnarsie, or Staten Island,
on Jewish holidays—
and I had the good sense
not to take anyone with me:
a truant should have no accomplices,
I was on the flag squad,
terrified of gangfighting,
the Nits and the Jollystompers
were recruiting, and I had decided,

in the deep reservoirs of the soul,
much like you seated here
resonate in the amplitude of this oasis,
which is sited on an old Egyptian-style
reservoir: and so I drank.

Miss Brooks and I shared the classroom
at Brooklyn College for a course taught
by Allen Ginsberg, and during q & a
a 50-year-old lieutenant from the Nits
stood up and complimented me
for surviving the street wars
(I had left our ancestral home on Lafayette
Avenue in 1951, the year of Willie Mays);
in 1947 there was a huge blizzard,
and in 1948 a hurricane that took
many of the chestnut trees
outside my bedroom.
In Los Angeles my neighbors
were bombing the homes of newly
arrived black interlopers
but 'geography is fate' said Heraclitus:
leaving all I knew in this city
made me a poet, the causality
of all that inner chatter.

You should ask me why writers steal
and for what purpose?
My preacher ancestors used to say
to be a good liar you have to have a good remembrance:
poets are good remembrancers.

I see your parents, teachers, family, friends
sitting on their remembrances:
talk to them and let them talk for you:
in our communities there is gumbo ya ya,
everybody talks; we are storytellers,

and we sit on and must harvest
in the nest of parlance and song
canonical stories, and sing them robustly:

words are not like music, though they are related,
much like relatives are related
without your active choice; but you can choose
your ancestors: this is the legacy of the library.

Mr. James Baldwin, essayist and writer from Harlem,
Henry James, and the library, cautioned us:
artists are here to disturb the peace.
He was not speaking of druglords, rap artists,
video kings, street peddlers;
he was describing our psychic condition
'by virtue of the absoluteness
of his estrangement from his past,'
that image beneath the threshold
of social hierarchy. Veblen
warned us about 'trained incapacity'
and we are lucky for his investigations.
Writers tell you, over and over,
that you cannot appropriate
squatters' rights, through piracy,
murder, scrupulous cunning:
you must love; that is the forecast
and the aftermath of your inheritance.

Technologists cannot be your shamans;
yet you can drink from this very oasis,
drink from what was once a city reservoir
given by the city that you might gestate,
germinate, metamorphose,
inside and outside, as a dome,
skyscraper, gridiron, skyline
and play, in the breaks,
as Satchmo instructed the Marsalis

Brothers, not with limos, hip-hop,
reggae, but with the brass
of the Constitution,
more honorable as it is amended
as an inclusive tool for Twain's
Jim and many a cracker peasant
with a steady paycheck on the assembly
line, and finetuning that creative
monotony for Henry Ford, Carnegie
libraries, and Wrigley's chewing gum,
"A Brighter Day" and bookcases,
collapsible stacks running for miles,
with breaks between solos, off-takes
and group effort harmonies
on the bandstand of ideas:
minstrel shows have allowances
built into the masquerade,
and as you impersonate
you find yourself, flourish
upsetting your own expectations,
not to mention others,
how simply you become 'An Arkansas Traveler:'

meeting life's terms but never accepting them
as a heartfelt attitude, as a personal stance,
as your honor to respect process
and to be your enjoyment,
in unarrested development
(is that a songtitle, a group, a label, a comic strip?)
your procedure, on the marble highway
of this palace, is procedure, is process:
heads/hearts/hands:

my relatives, many of them schoolteachers,
some alive in Brownsville, Bushwick,
Teaneck, Redhook, DeKalb, Throop,
were utility infielders in the Negro

Leagues, and making off-minor
theorems on the backfences
of praxis, cultural studies, and elegance:
wearing their Sunday clothes every day
at work and play, as reflex-theory:
begin with the heart and work outwardly.

As you paint yourself, taking readings
along the vernacular of the language
you speak, imitate, create, abandon,
remember the tensions of change:
improvise, study the movements,
don't get lulled by machines:
learn to drive them, and remain flexible
as an exercise in tinkering:
what is made is much less complex,
more tidy, less open-ended,
than the maker
who is, in every molecule, and valence:
an art form:
let us beautify
because it is our place
considering the sacred values
you represent. And give up information
freely, and this building has given,
with its librarians who guide,
sometimes create openings,
doorways, windows, vestibules,
hibernation satellites
for that inner music:
low, middle, and hi fi:
fidelity to that ideal
democracy which you represent
in every potential,
in all vestiges.

Mr. Ralph Ellison, the novelist,
essayist and trustee of American
constitutionalism, loved the frontier;
he was saddled, as every American
is saddled, with geography,
in his case: the territory,
Bessie Smith's territory, Indian
country, Oklahoma;
he watched freedmen, men and women
who had paid every price to be citizens
usurped from their earned positions.

He was the man who told me about
Roscoe Dungee, publisher of the Black
Dispatch, which kept its own archive
on the progress of the race;
it should not surprise you that the health
of democracy is insured by the participation
of its citizenry, no matter where the placement:
conscientious service for the general good
is always insured in the particular,
so be your own agency.
Mr. Ellison wrote his novel without the article,
INVISIBLE MAN; we are always negotiating
the seen and heard with the unseen
and the unknowable: the quest is knowledge
and aptitude for application of the music;
as to effort, the process is to make it,
emphasis on make; you were my clear winners;
believe me, I loved you all.
Mr. Ellison wrote his novel as an act of love;
writers are entrusted with the sacred history of the earth,
and much of that history is aesthetically based;
at the highest frequencies, not to mention whole notes,
vernacular art and artmaking is process:
bring your experiential tools and your transcendent antennae.

In America we fight hardest for our beliefs in the possible:
don't abdicate, provide, enhance, hold on!

> **Postscript:** Moving to the front of the NY Public Library,
> between the two lions carved from pink Tennessee
> marble, I talk with a man from the Caribbean:
> he says to me "I have two valedictorians, two girls,
> who attend different schools; I have nine children."
> Pride is too brief a term for his endearment;
> he is grateful; I tell him about the nine muses
> who reign over the arts and sciences; I tell him
> nine lives is better than one; his wife poses between
> her daughters, leaving a place for the father,
> insisting I pose next to them. I think of Frederick
> Douglass, who wrote his own autobiography,
> counseling Lincoln to be better than he knows
> how to be, as events, heartache, methodology,
> weapons, shape him: when the lions write history
> the lions will be king, and the kingdom will hear
> those illustrious, democratic muses,
> bringing up the future, promise, fresh water to drink.

––––––––
LEGEND OF JEANNIE TURNER
––––––––

The Kennedys came to Mullens
                              for speed on the dancefloor
the Irish slow on the upbeat
                    of big band maneuvers
unless political
          still they sent for Jeannie

champion breakdancer
        of the lindyhop
            who could also canvas
clean house with the overflow
          of advance-personnel
who were not advanced
        even on the Iowa battery
              of tests taken
and given up for lost
        even for Catholics
            the Irish Mist
flowing in Black Eagle Hollow
          with a constitution
              for freemasonry
which was the spell
      of Jeannie Turner
             before she took issue
quit school to raise her foursome
         and still outcampaign
tidewater clientele
       in every precinct that matters:
               what is legend?

Simply to be on call at trial
         to count ballots
            not stuff them
and do the world's work
        at parade rest
            which is no parade's end:
In Matewan
     organizers
       true and vagrant
           had to swim a swift stream

fully dressed
        to eat another day
                on the boardinghouse roll
                        as film

yet this is the world
            people live to write
                  to testify
                    at hearts

the lowly black widow
            in her web
                is the intricate trope
                    uttered

as legend
        which is her truth
                on any homespun urn
                    of graphite
                        or marble

TCAT SERENADE

30th anniversary of MLK, Jr.'s killing;
the cure to come

the wound of race as metaphor
in Seamus Heaney's TCAT

what he calls Homer's Ghost
and where the black heart of hope

resides in future
in the arc of history

as dramaturg, as bard, as sage
as only in a lover's hold

where rape incest
miscegenation

can be embraced as play
as useless curiosity

the anthropologists
store up as details

for the compass
of compassion

as prism
understanding

action
morality

grace
under extreme pressure

art
life

4 Little Girls
notes from a Birmingham jail

can be the cure at Troy
Philoctetes

with bow that never misses its mark
will break the arc

and let the other
speak

SHERLEY ANNE WILLIAMS: 1944–1999

Worshipped
in the fields

sometimes
in darkness

heat
at highnoon

killing fields
but after water

fluorescent
crops

braceros
picked

you sent me a tape
short and full

of healing music
(I copied it for my mother)

put you in every book
I could read or write

remember
your commentaries

at public
tables

in and out
of the university

outtakes are best
your heart a map

ancestors
weeping

CHLOE: BLACK PASTORAL LUMINOUS

---

for Toni Morrison

"especially one beloved"

Her father's favorite; and her mother's;
you hear chorale in that voice,
and in her handwriting, deliberately
illegible, its **hairlike** curlicues
oregano spores atop a poached egg
and 'down the long walk' on Howard's
campus, a delicacy, as words floe
in the carriage of the ancestors,
under heavy load, yes, but prehistoric
in their amplitude: you feel this
in this woman's presence, a girl
never in her life, but childlike,
fecund as in the making of words
in a symphony of sacred names:
lioness on the hunt, and in the kill.

I mention kill because we lunched
on her credit card discussing Shaka,
an epic narrative I was unable to write,
having just fathomed Senegambians

and negitos in cosmic opposition,
a paradox for BLACK BOOK, GIANT TALK
and the Lorraine Motel, which reminded
any foundry worker about Sweet Lorain,
driving wheel to workers' compensation,
a blues unsullied by rice fields:
barges carrying freight as immigrant
command, refugees of the ores,
and making plates of toxic steel
in the nation's skyline, an iron grace
she captures on her father's watch.

Re editorial control, caustic interviews,
and seminars, up close, where tapestry
is inner landscape, brute logarhythms
of unspeakable delights, the face of your kindreds,
on the Hudson, embers; in Paris, sparks;
Oslo majestic byply to play by:

I heard you step into a paradise
at the crossroads of muddy guitar;
we will pause at muddy: in painting
a bright watercolor now out of focus,
on the strings, a clarity never
to be erased. I put my hands on the stencil
of your rectitude: it was a choir of one,
as unity is preachment
at the waterfall of this nocturne,
stellae as bright as day.

HANDMADE BOOK ON THE THEME OF THE BELOVED

(And I should say
                on the theme of
                                the beloved

a child of the book
                whose fingers
                                weave tapestries

as remembrance
                week by week
                                under perfect
                                                instruction

as guide to
        'happiness'
                all we ever know
                                of the body

hers
    enshrined
            in that tee shirt
                        at vespers
                                calling me

as epiphany
            to the book
                    which could be sacred
                                in unrecorded
                                        play)

PIGEON

Females for sure; Nantucket
ferry to Martha's Vineyard

to attend a wedding,
perhaps read a nuptial blessing

but in the wind in the sun
on Friday, in a crowd

cars below move by reservation
but walk-ons are almost free

which is the attitude of pigeon
scurrying for corn on the top deck

and not about to fly off
when freebies are available

even without the asking;
I have a handcraft invitation

for this coupling
with proper family names

"Nantucket" the first ferry
Frederick Douglass took in 1841

disallowed from riding indoors
in unamended prohibitions in the north

on the same ferry line I park in,
an auxiliary tank, on wax fiber;

marriage on a new moon
by sidereal calculation

which is what he sought
in his five visits over forty years

making an argument for citizenship
so that none would proffer chains:

on the sanctity of matrimony
attendant to vows only a bird could make

ferrying on the topside of dross
all that is precious deep below

and at anchor cars, trailers, buses:
cellphone conversations as tryst

the ferry backing into the stall
for another maneuver across

an isthmus as virginal as isobars
in a binding needle of pigeon

ARTIST ON A CELLPHONE (YADDO)

In sweats, eating her hair,
she squats near the red fire hydrant

without a lunchpail at noon
the shorthand of the tennis court

a drizzle of privacy
the net Frost cautioned

it is a dance of sorts
a body training

for epiphany of pines
hidden behind lilac bushes

a week from the Travers
perhaps her reception digital

we have this on film
frame by frame

the sources of light
nothing like Rumi's fire

yet talk of the earthquake
so near the Bosphorus

could be the conversation
storm surge near Corpus Christie

a proverb is appropriate
Silence, too, is talk

VOTE (PROVIDENCE)

On Broad @ 7 A.M. across from PO
across from Gilbanes powerhouse alley

at this hour you can park in the lot
pass a man in tears struggling with his name

a signature without an address
the six propositions FOR according to Providence Journal

You are finished in five minutes if you can write your name, not hispanic,
    not wayfaring stranger poor

but you are all of these in spirit
passing the employ of your would be playmate   adept at unctions evermore

the nation prays into the secrecy of the machines
with no choice any choice from where I sit: a vast field of poverty

in a St. Jude mantra of the inner city
with my newly found sticker "I Voted"

pinned to my lapel jacket too thin to protect our windward traffic
to think about the employed who employ themselves workward

into the zone Gandhi entreated in another caste voluntary creed
"reflections while going to vote"

"to give pleasure to a single heart
by a single act is better

than a thousand heads bowing in prayer"
my ear to the chest leewardly set to the throbbing heartwork undone

---

MARILYN

Small hands small feet
in a tent

commodious
with handwriting

to match
sultry voicings

of the inner work
her privacy

right out front
in her demeanor

a weakness for opera
the aria

at close range
all she can stand

and she can stand plenty
sing to her

let her come to you
and camp

TATTOO

Though a simple rose under your skin
I look up the bugle ritual of recall

for sailors to regroup—soldiers at parade rest
and your sister who could not read as a child

needing you for sustenance—now you want it removed
Copenhagen (for me)   is Tivoli   played by Dexter Gordon

His love for that city—broad and low in balladry
for making the sound of recall   a lullaby

with his name on it—he would love to see your tattoo
his magic at composition   a call to Basie/Ellington

Hamp   and two full days of practice at seventeen
with the makers of bebop—just off the train from LA

the son of a doctor   whose doctoring gave such a smile
in the lower registers he was Mr. "Blue Note" (tenor)

he would venture his signature on conventions ROSE
and turn courtly in the madrigal—play you a hymn

and take you to his church   (which was always the road)
so you know why you came from the north—a town

just out of sight from Copenhagen—and in this poem
provided your sister that special speech of signals

so the faerytale of being pricked into song
just under the skin   was the song of a tent show

the tattooist fully sober   and without shaky hands
and just beneath the surface of your blood

Cezanne's Polynesian sorcerer—so genial in profile
that eating your salad is a school of painting

primal in the garden of the artist's magic circle
where every gesture is the canon of tattoo

────────

COPENHAGEN

────────

Tivoli a song of youth
by Dexter Gordon

there is no catchin' up
on what has been missed

'Round Midnight
night trains you should be on

ferry you cannot fathom
except as transit points

Rostock, East Germany seminar
in touch with secret police

as in zones
on visas detachable

so you can travel
the free world apartheid-class

what is it about this woman's touch
that makes all of me at attention

too many words he said
too much anger she said

right next to *Out of Africa*
every high school teacher Danish

in the land of *off minor*
came to pay tribute to black literature

only in Stockholm *An American Dilemma*
meeting Myrdal "how's Sterling?"

Dear Old Stockholm by Miles Davis
in the old section in the elevator *out of nowhere*

illicit pandemonium sidereal squalor
a cautionary tale in gnostic symmetries

you could administer *all the things you are*
with more than your mouth *so let the good times roll*

our child in your arms
in the Yaddo swimming pool

whose body *Citation*
cannot be denied?

stay away from him your mother cautioned
and you obeyed with Rilke's Angel

so who is the catcher on the Rhine
in what Cathedral the dragon in temple

Genever
Beethoven's sonatas in both your hands at once:

NOTES ON OUR RESIDENT HUMANIST:
MAHLER B. RYDER, 1937–1992

A moving van with your name on it,
all sides equal to a smokescreen,
all colors equal to a holiday greeting
of "The Cat" by Ulli,
an original design.

Now you are your Black Regiment
camped in the ice of Fannie Copeland's
homeownership policy
as written in the vestiges
of Swansonville plantation,
the pictorial walkthrough
of companions of the living trust
Susan Bellaire, helpmate, guide,
seamstress of "equipment for living."

Your medal of honor is a tablet
to ingest for indigestion:
it is licorice for the voice
when laryngitis hamstrings
even you in front of your illustrations,
the very self you've made out of string,
marvelous string,

from boxes in Bullocks:
this is the full dress
of the body at attention
in "Special Forces:"
it is the artwork that accedes almost nothing to life
"by any means necessary,"
but is spectacular on jumps
into the canopies
so rife and immaculate
with unknown fauna and birds
that drawing them
confounds Mr. John Muir
out for a bothersome stroll
in a camouflaged parachute:
it causes speculation
on black men liberating
German prison camps
while the inmates sang,
in unison, "Negro" spirituals.

You don't begin to understand
"Buddha," not to mention Buddhism,
until you're on a forced landing
at Katmandu, 12 thousand feet above
sea level, in January;
for the first time can see
as clear as kente broadcloth
Mt. Everest; then, leaving
the airport, armed soldiers
who cannot read the Tibetan
prayers they're paid
to intercept on rugs:
these rugs worshipped in thin air,
refuse to be Chinese,
refuse the resonant grease
of the sheep that carry them home.

We are reading the pamphlets
from the NEA minority grant proposal
guidelines you have written:
"art," which is what humanity is,
  being worked upon by the elements
  as in elementary Douglass school
'save your paper program;'
  sciences: for the will to dominate
  the eye of wonder, to calibrate,
"to record" the secret messages
  of the periodic table,
  mountains of the moon, depths
  below even the "equator;"
  humanity, as in Lynchburg,
  where the sheriff of the county
  is bowlegged, knockkneed,
  hairlipped, raised on raisinbran,

  turning out, even of the soaps,
  so he can make an arrest.

We must start with an argument,
  gingerbread man
  of the black keys of the 88;
  to be self-taught
  is to be self-loved,
  arrogant, dressed to kill,
  precise in speech,
  even on College Hill
  afflicted by the asthmatic inhalator,
  ancestor to the Xerox machine—
  in a word, "obsessive,"
  put together too tight,
  too tightly wrapped
  to ever be completed
  in greasepaint, tabernacle,
  adagio song-choir.

We will take your seminar
in behavior at boardmeetings,
panelist more arcane
than mahogany brass,
antique arc light of the autobahn,
flicking lights in the passing
lane without a whisper,
alive, in special forces,
with your foot on the gas.

You are study in the windowledges
of Hamburg just before Mardi Gras;
you are bad humored
on the subject of plantation,
from whence your grandmother walked,
at fourteen,
indulgent in the motion picture
of soaps, the handheld collage
in the kitchen, where grandma cooked your favorite apple pie.

You are Jim Marshall's running buddy
lost on the field of pigskin
ambling on TV in the wrong direction
for the Minnesota Vikings;
It is "Jim" who threw you bodily
downstairs at East High;

it is he that remembers Unitas;
it is you traversing the new Rose
Garden in the deep park of pioneer
city facing the due west sunset
on the Big Ten Jamboree:
Big "Jim" Parker's
singlehanded battle
in the pit
with Iowa's Calvin Jones,
"Cal" from Steubenville,

gridiron killer
of Hawkeyes,
of Wolverines.

Your meditations on the exquisite
intricacies of light on the penumbra
of Mapplethorpe's flowers—
perhaps a bit confused
over stems hanging
out of the pantsuits,
a waste of a good gabardine cloth.

You have problems
with hidden taperecorders
in the drawers
of the chairman
of the Black Heritage Society;
you are buried in the dictionary
of "freehold" land,
the sacred manna of the masons,
odd fellows, conjure men,
griots, harmon mutes,
mandolins, headrags;
you have problems with low art,

highbrow art, haryou,
Adam Clayton Powell's
white fraternity at Colgate,
Palmolive Shaving Cream,
Black PowWow Summits,
"the talented tenth."

You are fascinated with Joe Gans,
the Brown Bomber,
Sugar Ray, Thelonius Monk,
Sassy Sarah's piano player,
as if Sarah couldn't play box
herself;

you got problems with full tones,
quarter notes, half-nelsons,
half notes, puddin' rock,
apple blossoms that grow through skeletons
in cemeteries;
turn off that record player,
videotape, straight 8, 16 mm
photoscan, synthesizer,
acoustic resonance
polyurethane
obstacle course.

Some light comes from "antagonistic
cooperation," strobelight
and roulette wheel
of the Republic,
and we have gone to war
over strategies
and the ego drive.

In the boxing ring
along the walls
of gallery, outhouse,
and drawing room,
we process
all that is real
with valiant allusions
to the truth of what we know.

And we know this:
we are what we make;
it is the process
that gives up the glow
and mutant force
toward the true image.

We tell that truth
in infinite durability,
and the timely deed.

We have stepped inside
your strategic timezone,
the zone of timeouts:
maker of the moving veins,
or solitary songsters,
gleeclub of our mutual will:

We stand up to sing
through your destruction.

OSTSEEBAD AHRENSHOOP

for Horst Hohne

You have asked the impossible
                          and I have given it
your bright "Romantic" eyes
                          of your period
like the basalt
              of a seminar
                          on Yeats
                              on Whitman
with an intro-rejoinder
                    to the state
                          in argot
                              in slam

dinner was exquisite

        with French wine

                you could not get

                        at duty free

and on the ferry

        I saw your countrymen

                quiver

                   abandoning

                      Denmark

for a green train

        and a greener uniform

                and at the checkpoint

I turned my passport

        face down

            and would not

                list the books

I HAD BROUGHT

        FROM HOMELAND

                You asked

                   in Rostock

                      if I would

                        sermonize

on my people

        no matter

          the art

            and get close

                to Keats

                  as an alien

physician

        positively

            incapable

              of broken

                conceits

                  in his letters

and at this resort

        I have been commanded

                to another checkpoint

refusing

      to go

        one step

           in that direction

              my translator

                  from Prague

was detained

      at the border

         and lost his passport

              in East Berlin

and was told

      to stay put

        in his hotel

          and not to move

                into prosody

in his case

      a close study

        of the meters

          of Whitman

            his taps

              among dead

"workers"

      leading

        from the body

          of A. Lincoln

            as lilacs

              as urns

and so

      in his depression

        at not being

          able

           to move

              off-site

I took him
              by one lapel
                          an icebucket
                                      in one hand
                                                  Perrier champagne
in the other
            and broke
                      in *brut*
                              as if Koln
                                        was a perfume
                                                      the church
plangent
          as purgatory
                      and spoke my piece
                                        on integration
                                                      black-American-
style
        taking cue
                  from Thomas Mann's
                                    Klaus
                                          who saw
                                                  no end
                                                        to evil
affixing
        Slavery
                as John Hope Franklin
                                    would report
                                                less evil
                                                        than Reich
at Checkpoint Charlie
                        where I had been
                                            behind enemy lines
                                                                moments

notice

    in the sights

        of guards

           who had shot

               women and children

                   on orders

and I walked out

        to that point

           having toured the West

               avoiding the East

and found two brown soldiers

           from Cedar Rapids

               with Iowan accents

both under twenty

        I handed each

           a book I was carrying

               in broken parlance

of musicians

        I had copied

           their phrasing

             so mirthful

               honest

                 blue

that I confessed

        I had caught

           the train

             in Marion

               Iowa

               leaving

                 the workshop

in a gloss of sleet

        sick with the flu

           anxious for the mountains

               Chinese

immigrants

    had traversed

        in Coleridge fashion

            but without a khan

                to comfort

marginalia

    and those two

        border ruffians

           from Iowa

              grinned

                as only a

                  kinsman

can greet

    the divide

        that springs

           in a fence

             or a post

                of Black Hawk's

                  teepee

on the Des Moines

    River

        on the West

           Branch

              of a Pow

              Wow

                I gave them each

      in paper

        who'd loved

DEAR JOHN, DEAR COLTRANE

Checkpoint Charlie

      as Charlie Chan

          at Massey Hall

              in Toronto

alias
    Yarkbird
        blow bird
            on the wall
                at cultural
                    divide
                        which kept
                            us

free
  for artistry
      when nothing
          else
            could ring
               that hammer
                  song

no anvil
    poached
      in Veblen
        of Schurz
          could tempo
            the music
              of Juneteenth

blue as a tin
      penny
        finishing
          nail
            on Sterling
              Brown's
                study
                  of the pause

in the heroic

        couplet

            he'd worked

                against

                    conceits

                        of end-rime

                            words

in neoclassical

        plays

            closed couplet

                to run-on

                    couplet

                        Romantics

chose

    to stay

        out of prison

            rhetorical sense

                and meter

                    quite fit

for epigrams

        "Be not the first by whom the new is tried;/
nor yet the last to lay the old aside."

                    At this resort

                      Horst Hohne

I take

    the Browning look

            to stay

                wide open

                    in a field

                      as checkpoint

to my ancestors

who learned

to read

and write

as homilies

to kinfolk

born near

Massey Hall

and Parker's Mood

the scansion

of Coltrane's Sound

with resort pay

at not taking

order

except

in hours

of praxis

off and on

the bandstand

where even Whitman

stole the idea

of American

Grand Opera

from slaves

who could dance

and stretch

their talk

beneath

the threshold

into the upper

registers

of the American

idiom

I preach

because

my mother

taught me to

     read

       the classics

         in a broken

           tongue

             which could be

'memorable speech'

      had Auden

        left Hayden

         alone

           in blank

             verse

               "Middle

Passage"

   Amistad

     in that deft cage

        he will

        sing

         true   too

RIBS

for Maria van Daalen
Cuirt Festival, Galway, Ireland

We are already in the news
          though not the *Irish Times*
and Seamus has not reviewed us;
               still Black Bush
springs onto the table,
          after McDonagh's common fare
and Catharina Maria is no longer hungry
             though ready to dance.
Beneath all the "feminine aspect" labels
             is an ample freelance woman
her song broken and mended by peacemaking
             only Dutch translation can cure.
We will go by ferry to the Aran Islands
             with or without the sun
there will be no news to speak of
             yet to speak the idiom of poetry
is true translation
          I am sorry about the siege of Iowa City
when you were set upon by thugs
             who thought you were gay
                  male

transvestite
your leather britches
          blonde streak
             spike
            lifting
             you in high boots

to the infirmary;

          soon

               you had to go home

                     to Tinke

                         and be her mother.

Sacred callings:

          mothers;

               mine taught me to read

                     THE ARABIAN NIGHTS,

taught me to call my sister, Katherine,

               Shaharazad,

                     as no opera

in this world could capture,

                 nor her mother and mine

                       Katherine Louise

as no Johnson girl had ever been

                 inheritor of the *Johnson lungs.*

I would touch your ribs

               with a poetic kiss

                     your first trip to Ireland

would symbolize

               and you would continue

                   blithely

                   as yourself

                       in folklore

which is reality

          not the persona

               in a script

                   no one has heard;

to see you

        astride

        a brief encounter

                 outside the Atlanta Hotel

                     in Galway

those ribs to kiss
                    in words
                                in flesh
is a sacred
            dance
                    leaving eden

CHARLOTTE AND NATHAN EXCHANGE: 50TH ANNIVERSARY

". . . be advised
My passport's green
No glass of ours was ever raised
To toast the Queen"
—Seamus Heaney, *from "An Open Letter"*

(Charlottesville, VA)

As king and queen to epiphany
you should go to Nevis for sun
Alabama for shade (the wizard's advisements);
banking and fugitive criticism
money and theology the sanctified;
deadly combinations
both Yonkers and the Bronx
(when the Bomber was still champion)
the sport of bones
now our wishbone
and therefore unbreakable.
Once, on the Erie canal,
you were both on iceskates:

1946 surely
surrounded by siblings/goslings:
instantly Uncle Tom's Cabin
comes to mime: H. B. Stowe/A. Lincoln
the ice of dancing
(a twin set of islands)
to Canadian freedom
(or is it the Caribbean?):
all skaters were geese,
and because on the ice
and not aloft
very unYeatsian,
not a word from Lady Gregory;
the war was over
yet Sister Goose
(mistress of folksay)
was swimming on the lake.

Nonce for the theme of reflection,
the mirror "After Long Silence"—
talk after rootbeer and cider:
the framed tales of each self
as themselves,
as an endtable
to two hearts
lured into the other's notes
still brisk and alive
in the singing.

CHARLOTTE TO NATHAN

This is a genus Nobel
but it is under protest

doing research on FFOV
in Orange Courthouse

I was told 'go back to the UVA
archives; consult family letters...'

though James Randolph Braxton
catered the Chase Manhattan

catered the meal for the wizard
in 1903, (then he died)

his obituary spread out like a French menu:
five fingers of the hand

all Manhattan born
bought two houses a block apart

(the suburbs) Brooklyn, for his two daughters
cut loose three sons

corresponded with the wizard
on foreign investments

Jay Gould sent his oldest to Paris
to manage his personal effects

nothing but the crash
could bring him home

this menu a framed tale
to this evening's snails

so let us toast to better music
sermonizing Adam Clayton Powell

in a Hazel Scott sonata
in the Harlem pigalle

St. Phillips vestrymen
were at attention

uptown on the well-kept streets
the pews were ready as tender

tintypes were approved
jobs were plentiful if you could read

and read you did as the catering
caboose made the cash for Brooklyn

saving for the public library
that was the reservoir in which we strolled

NOTES ON THE HOPI

The work to be done is not to copy
their displacement, not to brood

on the economy of suffering
or name the dreadful facts

of their distemper:
it is to copy peace

you cannot find in the notations
of self that won't let you go

into their songs
a plateau of starstruck

lamentations in dust
on the sprinkle lining

the children sing
at Jonestown

a book by Wilson Harris
from the archipelago [Womb of Space]

of my great grandfather from Guyana
(Harris who looks like my kin

my dead Uncle Barrett Johnson
who drove a foursome

nearby Four Corners
on the River Road

outside of Utica
near Rome, New York in 1949)

you remember Saint Jude
his mettle, my uncle

waiting for rescue
freeing his body

out of the treeline wreckage
where three passengers had died (not Aunt Ella Mae from

"Juneteenth"—born in Austin, Texas, her daughters Michon &
Cynthia my only blood cousins in this world)

before him: renegades from Griffis Air Force Base—
Hopi prayers as starstruck rainfall

We are the ones we have been waiting for
We are the ones we have been waiting for

CRITICAL MASS

for Brian McHale

We are reading James Wright's obituary
in the Martins Ferry, Ohio library

Liberty Kardules, his first wife,
mother of Franz & Marshall

sticks in the craw
and "Arlington" comes into view

JAW's middle name
more than any battlefield

in the national suckhole;
with no sign on the Wheeling bridge

we stumble into Human Services Welfare dorms
and look for directions, and speech,

from the toothless black woman
you say is from Pittsburgh

where you were born
while JAW says "my Ohioan"

led to the portals of American Legion Hall
across from the library, bright Saturday,

Kwame's day in the Gold Coast
where this Akan woman probably came from

the teeth are really to be found
in Edith Anne Wright

JAW's second wife
and no doubt "Jenny" JAW's muse

mentioned in the poem about the WPA
Swimming Pool, and before long we are there

two ducks on the lip of the pool
undrained and posted by four lifeguard stands

WW I Memorial, the park, basketball players
in scrimmage, picnic table on concrete bandstand

and benches for the listeners
ghostdancers we do not sit down

the Ohio River City of Martins Ferry Water Treatment Plant
across from Shreve High Stadium "Purple Riders"

high hurdles on an unraked track no horseshoe
can break in the trot of Wheeling Pittsburgh Steel

still operating on the harbinger's gums
God bless you in the name of "Arlington" citizen-pilgrim

HEMINGWAY'S ICEBERG

In the news
B10A

the shipping lanes
by Canadian satellite

its infrared data
iceberg topography

twenty four by forty eight miles
horizon daylight

smaller bergs
scattered powdered sugar

in warm water "crumbs"
the ice shelf penguins

since 1992 N current
en route to South American coast

Hemingway wrote standing up
his royal on telephone books

in the heart of downtown
Havana (his hotel)

so much below the surface
of his iceberg

a nine to one ratio
to the Cuba gold

he drank
when not fishing

no sugar so sweet
as what we taste and can't see

SAINT DOLORES
(PHILLIPS EXETER ACADEMY)

Abyssinian,
foggy bottom rose:
the sable story
of morass,
the morpho

come to quiet
costume,
life, and alive
in the pit
of New Hampshire.

She could not start here;
privileged larvae
of the few
have eaten
at her plummage.

She would be old,
older than they who want
to wear her clothes,
skin of cheetah,
drape of upas tree:

this is their christening
to all memory,
every song she sings.

"DAYS REMAINING"/BLOOM'S DAY, DUBLIN

we are at the end of the book (and doing nicely)
so many begun   never to be ended

the tome of feeling   'on the sea'   neptunian
(still we must go back to the bow/symbolic/bow)

loved the full day of Molly's bloom
loved her cuckoldry religious to a fault line

in the catechism   the Latin verses vulgate in its Irish
tongue affixed to the magical place   crossroads

on the body template   each gender marooned
angry with festering wound   the snake endlessly

poisonous as all myths are until a wily brigand
steals into the bedroom of sorcerer or sphinx

where no riddle is undone   conundrum solved
as all platonic equations   aristotelian tools

"man is a storytelling animal" women worse
preternatural genomes   unity of the curse

FREUD: LESSONS ON BOUNDARIES

3% jews in town: Jacob (the father) a wool salesman
with seven siblings he loses mama's care to tb

his daynurse arrested for theft
alone now in the heart   darkness in the midst of vision

all bad solutions to the marriage problem
Nurse   Church   Phobia   a frozen tintype

hates train-travel   hates cocaine   hates cigars
yet succeeds by losing   the Nazis   whose parents stay behind

you must move on   the oedipal trauma
most reasonable in the feet   old swollen feet

unraveling that unexcavated self (1856–1939)
'erroneous universal law some provinces ignored'

the woman of instinctual emotions is the turnkey to the id:
male bonding   the camps   to come   as floes

wherein the spectral geese are suddenly found
phosphorescent:paradox:primal:irony:writ:large!

GEORGE J. MAKARI BLUES

'your health is the floor you stand on—'

Student, counselor, doctor, friend
are you paying attention to your own advice?

I ask this from the providential corner of Wilbour Hall
"Egyptology"   a world of arcane musing   and books

the mantra of "Use Trouble" most recently culled from Jacob Lawrence
is exhibit of bright and fundamental hues deeply etched in your soundbank

for sound is the sonic recall of your rounds
among patients I can never visualize except in the vedas

perhaps Beirut when we talked hours about the 'lupusofAbraham'
transfigured in the seminars of the Brown medical school program

your parents Christian   Muslim   Jew as only doctors can be
in the veils and transparencies of the book

you have carried your efforts in to the private space of my relatives
and come back with diagnostics predictable to the nth degree

I have not expected such dedication but I have reveled in it
now I bequeath you to tend your own spirit in your own name

and none other   remember our dinner at the Plaza when I was on expenses
the meal glorious on and off the menu for I had spoken to the chef

of that very day's kill dragged from the expressway of vittles
"you must not eat yourself up in devotion to the craft of healing"

though you listen to TELL ME HOW LONG TRANE'S BEEN GONE
in sacred spots of the dial   each spot a location of music

your mentor and friend hosting the narrative of *intentional suffering*
a concept you have pondered and acted upon in every sonority

Coltrane himself went to the highest mode of supreme love perhaps in
    "Alabama"
certainly "Dear Lord"   "Acknowledgement"   all versions of "Spiritual"

I sit with you this very morning, Paul Robeson's natal day, conjuring
the voice of existence [intentional suffering] and feel your strength

wither and come again aftermath of the battlefield of 9/11 our next
migration series

again Hayden's 'no place for any child' in his "Year of the Child"
to place you in the middle of your vestiges with no insurance: history

FOR US begins in murder and enslavement not discovery reminding you
just this once "it is the man/woman outside who judges"—that the most

sacred care chooses you and not the reverse still love yourself
first, my friend, then the world:

"I was a hidden treasure and I loved to be known
I was a hidden treasure and I loved to be known"

SONGBIRDS (HABITAT)

whole registers of song
mostly in the mornings

territory a heartbeat
for keeping the race alive

race a habitat of attraction
the long whole notes of action

sometimes the silent ones raise another's
one can only know who roosts via mothers

He waited in his monotones through lunch
cascading from the highs to scrunch

hungry at the royal roost of song
appetite for the great along

"PONTA DE AREIA" [BRAZIL]

I have my *cachaça* and hear the sea
with the salt though the tone is interior music

sound of the musical bow ritual of *capoeira*
new world martial art from Angola couched as slave guitar

the orchestral residue of '64 military coup
now alive in the pigalle district of Paris

we have sweetened 'a friend named "*Johnny Walker*"'
killing the invisible chops as you save your jack

to get back home to favella-samba die alone in Rio
After slavery was over **in 1888** the blues of monarchy

somehow innocently portrayed in the film "A Man and a Woman"
toned down in our country of beautiful places but falling down

who sing this tempo of the forest
each native goldmine **capoeira**

music protecting me but a child
adrift in this song of the sublime

to see the isthmus new lingua franca of the *tongue*
narrow passage of longing: **ponta de areia Brazil**

TAGORE (NOBEL, 1913)

From the sanskrit only jingles
if the west would tell it straight
but this is a Bengali poet
2000 songs to his poems
and in the west nothing sacred;

Shankar is not here;
we are missing the dogwhistle
in the permanence
of the Ganges;
my friend, Supreo Bonnerjee,
a brahman of the first order,
expert on Calcutta,
and loving the African in us

invites me to the family pot
in his kitchen; then off
to buy four saris for the four
women in my life,
in the charge of his wife,
her royal dot of henna
echoing the kama sutra
of daily bread in daily
worship of dynasty,
her husband's heart
older than the synagogue
and breaking at his own
funeral pyre, older than psalm
23 in memorial
to the ancients;
weaponry in every culture
notched by the Nobel
is our idiom of forgiveness.

Tigre, alive in the delta,
attacking from behind
and cunning beyond mangrove,
ascends to the great chain
of being, and becomes Tagore
or is it Yeats
locating his own mysteries
in the original
Arabian Nights:
loving the framed tale
of Mozart's high E or F
beyond the range
of any soprano

ON BRODSKY'S COLLECTED

"With all tenderness and affection"

Signature in a paperback
arresting your copious

annotations on "September 1, 1939"
(exegetical in the extreme)

extreme unction of the heart
such lucid heartwork without translation

bright bed and breakfast
in macabre Providence very unPoelike

for I have read your EnglishAmerican
(as you have read your RussianSoviet)

to a vast audience of scientists
in the graduated labs of Barus & Holly

a valiant pant across participles
the psychic hum of all lingua you intuited

"for language is the only homeland"
metaphysician of this psychograph an interrogation

sutures of blood and song
your generous taxonomies in cavernous secret vena cava

THREE POEMS: OCTOBER 17, 2004

for Katherine Haley Will

Lincoln, Abraham: American statesman and president
(1809–1865). Though Lincoln's collected writings are more
extensive than those of Shakespeare, the great majority
of his production was necessarily ephemeral speeches
and documents interesting only to students of political
history. A few of his works, however—The Springfield
Address, the Second Inaugural Address, and especially
the Gettysburg Address—have taken their place among
the common property of mankind. Lincoln was almost
entirely self-educated, and his literary models were
his early reading: Bunyan's Pilgrim's Progress, Defoe's
Robinson Crusoe, Aesop's Fables, and, above all, the King
James Bible. To these were added a special sort of frontier
homeliness and raciness acquired around the stoves of
country stores and in the rough and tumble of political
campaigning. Lincoln came early to regard his mission
as the defense and extension of human freedom. After
his series of debates with Douglass he commented to
a friend: "I believe I have made some marks which
will tell for the cause of human liberty long after I am
gone." During the war years he regarded the Civil War
as a test—for all the world to see—of the possibilities of
freedom's survival. In November 1863 (the year of the
Emancipation Proclamation), he spoke at Gettysburg
National Cemetery. He was invited to speak as an
afterthought, but the two-hour effort of the main orator
of the occasion is forgotten, while Lincoln's few sentences
are immortal. The Gettysburg Address answers those
who say that Lincoln used no rhetorical devices. For

all its difference from conventional rhetoric, it shows
most skillful alliteration, assonance, climax, balance, and
antithesis. More important, of course, is the march
of ideas in the simplest but best words to the solemn
cadence. In this speech Lincoln's simple diction, broad
humanity, and humble consciousness of his historical
mission combine to produce his masterpiece.
—The Reader's Companion to WORLD LITERATURE
    (Sterling A. Brown)

I. Archival Secrets of Mary Lincoln

She would speak in French with guests
particularly Charles Sumner

the scene of seduction of A. Lincoln
in the White House should also be in French

Carriage talk between the lovers while
visiting the wounded soldiers out of cask

confederates at table should lead grace
in Latin Greek (no Spanish French Portu-

guese but a map of southern hemisphere
will be timely) 'geography is fate' reminder

forget slavery as an industry focus on
Robert the son's campaign to stop union

organizing of George Pullman's porters
(the darkest ex-slaves after emancipation)

psychographs of this invisible obsession
will tell you much of why he treated

his mother so don't forget Studs Terkel's
interview with Ed Nixon organizer of MLK Jr.'s

Montgomery boycott Christian ministers
(Rosa Parks was Edgar Nixon's friend

before she got arrested) learn how to place
people before and after emancipation

remember Hayden's "The Dream" (1863) cadences
as whisper and shout of blues and laughter

Harpers Ferry treatise on Black Hawk at Iowa (hawkeye)
Lincoln was no saint but the best linguist writing his own speech

"I have sung to him beyond the grave   a capella
and he has come to me   alone across the canebrake"

II. AT THE SQUARE

Lessons in Proverbs: ENERGY ENGAGEMENT ENLIGHTENMENT

Crow flight: it is not for food
that the insides are created

presidential mindreading: today is yours
tomorrow belongs to another

what won't translate: wealth is a coat of thorns
without library faculty students   heartwork

the human heart is where we live
let it not be a walled city

WILL legacy: a malady of the eye: have patience
(a one-eyed woman does not thank Allah until she sees

another blind woman)
silence, too, is talk

even in facsimile there is no going back
except for essentials

[let the doing be the exercise
not the exhibition]

———————————

windows look out on Lincoln and a citizen
"Home of the Gettysburg Address"

the coming and goings of Thrift Shop Traffic
hispanic men and women in bright sweats

the cuffs of the American Red Cross
'the light around the portrait'

tourist capitol of Pennsylvania too close
to the Mason-Dixon line   typographical insult

to Lincoln University "out in the sticks away from site"
with alumni like 'thoroughgood' and James Langston Hughes

then a troop of students in yellow-hooded umbrellas
came wafting by   American cacophony of flags unannounced

but full of spunk 'walking through lightning'
as though waiting to be struck by wares emails (no archives)

"bending the knees isn't the only way to pray"
frontiers: geographical   intellectual   hierarchical

for the president knows essential American provisionals:
"art is an assault upon logic" (people are art forms all over)

III. The Secret Lore of Will's Presidency

With mastery of the collage   where to enter
she looks up again parataxis

the pattern of comprehension
original not to be explained

by a simple song   "Don't Explain"
even when sung by Lady Day with Pres

the nine muses come into play to play at kingship
(collage in the spirit of making)

calculus the solution of faultlines
in the nation's ethos toasts called for

and freely given: integration the one that counts
Stillness at Appomattox   Brown v. Board of Education

now transformed by luminous deeds at play
"density of felt experience"   Henry James called it

Father Abraham by runaways and contraband alike some maroons
the gambler who put certain pressure on the republic

by words and not too many of them   that calculus
which says (eloquently) "that of the personality"

as Burke and Bergson (also originals) foretold all
"equipment for living" consider death as time in metaphor

for artwork at the extremes of cognition
composition as headstart to abstraction

if one is to encompass the heart   her intuitive organ
of intellect with grand design   to improvise cunningly

in the act of being solo in grand execution (of the board)
of the group   its tribal sentience

her nuclear will   as Keats would have it   in his letters
"negative capability"   but fearsome too

her memorable speech   (more than promissory note)
again   her cunning   its aftermath   living-lore-exquisite

"the route to the ancestors courses through
the byways of the otherworld;

and it is only as she was called to membership
in that world that the past became affective reality."

ZEN: THE TRAINRIDE HOME TO THE WELCOME TABLE

In Memory of Gwendolyn Brooks, 1917–2000

We know you parsed your best and worst thoughts
on the train   so this is traintalk

the waiters are weeping
(in the chair car your baggage is at parade rest)

every book you did not write is at attention
(your family steadily on your mind   and steady on the trestle)

HOLD ON was your laterday mantra over kinship ties
(I remember the whole family at lunch in Providence Plantations)

your discretion at signing your own books   pamphlets   broadsides
in the "Harris Collection" after convocation you had given (lemons make
    lemonade)

was another entry in the travelogue above and below ground
"the bronzeville connection"   to holy water   ritual of cleansing after battle

arpeggio daughter of the sacred elements on our periodic table
mother of the exquisite phrase   break our hearts   with every heartwork

we will forgive the heartfelt but disrespectful trivia of salutation
a reading of "We Real Cool" by anyone but you as if you needed exegesis

when explication would do: you loved those sacrificial lambs
despite their carriage   as proper nouns   as active verbs   as declensions

(so much fieldwork among "your enemies" masquerading as friends)
lay my body down as only Lincoln could in the swiveltongue of inaugurals

yes, you were a "friendship train" in the argot of motown
so glorious the pen (and handwriting) as none other than our holy ghost
     champeen

at welcome table the ancestors presiding   too many children now wellfed
a little sorbet while peeping out the window (blinds or no blinds)

the south side of our equator "steady as the rock of ages"
Gwendolynian in the extreme unction of this tabernacletrain

tight quarters of the kitchenette on wheels
(Lord how those brothers could cook on short notice)

those sisters soothe as the songbirds strutting on air
(look homeward angel just a little ahead of the curve)

in the last pennantdrive of banquetry digestibles
when this code should be one syllable each crosstie junction

went down to the place to hide my face
(there's no hiding place down here)

on the levee   with the angels   to spread those gorgeous wings:
Zen   GWEN   key to the zone of understanding as universe the poet
     contemplate

THE FLIGHT HOME

I watched #292 last Wednesday as it circled into LAX
to a perfect landing   the blaze of the nose gear "dead slow"

as you recited the signs of London as a six year old
Glenice sent me picture of your kids and her kids

lost in the playground of backyards   when I thought I could protect you
(from what I had no inkling   but there was no foundation of love at home

and my parents knew it: I made up this deficit with 'sweat equity'
delusions I would not wish on anyone   certainly not "the beloved")

you were a day early on Jet Blue   an hour late on your natal day
just yesterday a friend thought your MYTH OF MUSIC was mine

because she had much chaos with her own father she did not consult the
    jacaranda treeline
which could have trellised a certain story   though she did get my f.o.i.a. file
    from the govt

which began in 1960 perhaps earlier before I went to Iowa with a draft
    notice instead of a passport to Paris
[I think you remember Paris which you spent on your 25th birthday: "don't
    you think your only daughter

ought spend her 25th birthday in Paris?"   with 2K and your travel
    documents: done
always knew what to ask for and how to get it Lyal and Ruth drove from
    Trona to meet Katherine and Warren

to protest the coupling that would produce you and four others   lots of
    wreckage and heartwork in that vehicle]

the parenthetical   which I studied in Hayden's psychographs   are freely
   given to you   my daughter

please decode such wages of love in the annals of flights home   after
   publicity
so the cover of your first novel will be of your choosing: you must fight for
   everything in the marketplace

                    and elsewhere
otherwise Jaxon Auden 'mei mei' jacaranda periwinkle
are paradoxical   chaos unharnessed by art crafted in unity   in desire

---

TATUM

I have recovered from your blindness
so fast your arpeggios

the world of Toledo is in slow motion
for you are holding back

from all your classical training
the image of Fats Waller frozen

in the blows that forced darkness
into cranial blows irreversible

you are your own orchestra
soft periods in your program

hard as the message of your countrymen
"please return safely to your kin"

for you are a patriot
no matter discrimination

the virulent embers classical
in your repertoir: Columbus

every enemy's empathy concerto
every friend a suite sonata

they say you loved *trains*
(gondolas locomotives a fuel line)

when you died in 1956
a whole cavalcade came with you

Robinson retired
Mays carrying his team

your love of baseball
in the *signs missed and missing*

_____

BASEBALL (ORB)

_____

Ballbearing at the center
stitch neither vertical

nor horizontal flight
of same 9 players on

either team alternating
over the points of a

diamond abrasive gemstone
Babe launched magic

of Walter Johnson who hit
absolutely nothing most

of the time time out
for Yogi's antics Jackie

taught the world how to
steal black as the ace

of spades which gets into
digging basepaths for slats

Marion who could fill a hole
Sparky very ugly Stengal

ungrammatical the Negro Leagues
a world apart magicians at all

bases the names Monarchs

Blacks Barons Grays Birds

a world of animal at the bit
Mays a Cobb at motorways

industrial strength foulpoles
up the middle a minefield at play

JOSH GIBSON (MASTER OF NATIONAL PAST)

Better than the Babes at his position
the bat lean and ugly the home run

his invitation to explore dominate
frighten the opposition who were not

fearless or feardriven they play each
other every day the whites on either

hand were special occasions sandlot
play barnstorming nothing with big

paydays Dean knew owners new black
owners knew more about talent pools

lost wages stadiums ballfields yet
when competition money demographics

reigned the best cashed in Rickey
first Red Sox family never Mays

the best of all turned away even Ted
hawkeye/splinter Williams knew patrols

playing with Dimaggios all around him
while Robinson seared everybody smarts

tactics attitude court-martial Rachel
(Gibson died before his time aneurysm

anomaly his own dominance when Paige
was kind or thought he was walking

away exploiting the marketplace then
Jack Doby broke the backs of rednecks

all feared Josh's bat he could do ugly
on and off the field left us early too

on the trestle of Jim Crow funeral cars
lies the body of Josh Gibson

BLACKJACK

1963;
we march.

I look our remedial
white windowed essays
from Pasadena
I will read tonight
and there you are visiting
three black sisters
excluded from official parade
"their skins unlovely."

Orange and Fair Oaks
to grow on
to the stadium
blocks where you stand
silent; I am silent—

Nodding I say
'47 high noon in the bleachers,
Cards in town,
you jog the outfield grass
lagging loose balls,
how you lofted their cream-
skinned signatures
over the white heads
where we sat pigeon-toed
circling their dugout,
how we carried your curled
name to our table
while your team cursed
your singed garters
on pennant flagged tongues.

As they saw nothing
but your teeth and eyes
we saw the jeering train
unwinding its sheets in Georgia,
your mail cringing with snake
juice spat in the Bronx;
and when you crossed
our borders we cheered
our black ace
of the marked deck of Westwood,
the bowl we stand in,
the counter where their salted
nuts stack in their vacuum cans.

We will not speak of broad
jumps over tracks,
yardlines of pigskin
jaunted, stitched white balls
spiked at your skull:
we will remember the found
sleep and meals you lost
running over bases
their pitchers feared covering,
balls you made them eat
now flowering from your son's
funeral car.

High blood pressure,
diabetes,
your eyes gone blind,
I will not answer.
I steal home
at your back
down the red clay road
of their stadium
recalling Rachel,

my own daughter,
on deck.

"Did he say Blackie?"
my brother said
of the white boy
in row G:
'Black Jack,
the gamble's taken,
the debt unpaid,
and the answer,
answered, still to come.'

LOOK BACKWARDS: HENRY AARON'S HAMMER

Recall John Henry's overtaking steam
drilled into the heads of fans kids

sandlots over the shoulder range
without theatrics remember Mobile

where Satchel lived McCovey Ozzie
Billie Williams Cleon Jones Agee

In Milawaukee Matthews came to pray
over Henry's 'on deck' stance afield

doing the impossible every day without
fanfare without losing his cap even

once but ounce by ounce a force
enforcing everything complete as model

few could follow hit run throw field
hit with power (the numbers piling up

on strange fields visitations all-star
games numbers where the ball carried)

hate hatemail threats commissioners
off the game of making records in attendance

homefield advantage turnstyles fans
of every stripe virulence kidtalk

his anvil was every day peruasion
of the opposition his teammates knew

he was complete from womb to tomb
in any field you care to plant a monument

you don't carry his glove bat shoes
you carry the fence and the ball goes over

A CENTENARY ODE TO EKE: THE DUKE OF ELLINGTON

"Fate is being kind to me. Fate doesn't
want me to be famous too young."
—Pultizer quote, 1965

UCLA Centennial Festival: 4 29 99

This is about the experiment; it is about a prize, a free gift,
a bundle of riffs, a tradition, and it is art

experiment is art and artful, strangers in the master's house
which the artisans built, perhaps invisible, perhaps quotable

the free gift most quotable: "I been down so long that down don't
worry me," so worrying the line is deft improvisation

in the White House the butler brings the proverbial news,
in manners table manners, the frontier now parlance for government

the governed semiliterate in European news, indigenous
grace, all meals to be eaten at parade rest in parade time

"East St. Louis Toodle-oo" and Black and Tan Fantasy
is the tensile rigorous blues-based mode to set

the visible darker side of life, with technical prowess
in the veiled brillantine of Negro American style

for we were never in a white country, despite the movies,
soundtrack minnows in sharkteeth our "Birth of a Nation"

a nation elegant, even in race records, even fantasy,
melodrama, quixotic sketches of anomalous charts

even that eatery in the country's airways, aircharts,
optimistic Elysian styles direct from the Civil War

as mimicry is sounded fantasy, is Fredi Washington,
Ethel Waters, Florence Mills, Ivie Anderson

heartwork in the kitchencabinets of the nation's ethos
and the nation's wares; worries the sacred songs as spiritual

all costumes iridescent in the transcendent
where even God and the angels, across continents, swing

the orchestra is sometimes late, very late, "but always on time"
Strayhorn chortled, redcaps from everywhere carrying the news

so much manhood eclipsed in rendezvous one-nighters
in all the dark communities of this world and elsewhere

Sophisticated Lady/ Satin Doll
Take the A-Train

Liberian Suite/ Latin American Suite/
Afro-Eurasian Eclipse Suite

Symphony in Black/ Anatomy of a Murder/
Paris Blues/ the Queen's Suite

Such Sweet Thunder/ Black Tan and Beige
"Come Sunday" featuring Mahalia Jackson a capella

A Drum is a Woman/ Afro-Bossa
Creole Love Call/ Harlem/ Caravan

"I love you madly" as signature
to bassline of the experts

the nation's blueprint as arpeggio-footage
on Movietone News, his men and women

alchemizing notes, harmonies, rhythms, melodies
in practice sessions on the sidecar of Pullman

in our gerrymandered American folk-operetta:
"do nothing till you hear from me"

"do nothing till you hear from me"
"do nothing till you hear from me"

"do nothing till you hear from me"
("and you never will")

RAY CHARLES ROBINSON   DEAD AT 73

Out on the Green at Brown You Sang
(Achebe insisted on his own tickets

honorand in wheelchair traditional
African   costume of 'Chief' of the book)

Anani Dzidzienyo   trustee of the Padre
protector of the flock   personal honor

guard   including the music at adjacent
table   amidst distinguished guests

white man with wrong dancecard   approaches
Padre   as swing man   to Ray's calendar

Anani stops Padre from speaking   or hitting
back   an incident in bad form

while escorting the Chief of books
(though THINGS FALL APART   cold on Brown's

savannah   **1764** Baptist beginnings   only
half-way back to Elmina

Cape Coast   'an outpost of progress'
Achebe wrote   on Conrad's intended)

Ray died of acute liver disease   classmate
of *Quincy Jones*   in Seattle   played

America's music   'up and down ballrooms'
stadiums   honky tonks   bedrooms   outhouses

"walked on water"   "I got a woman   way
'cross town' . . . she good to me"   every day

rock and glare   behind sunglasses
(fools fumbling for 'tips' in custommade

clothes)   nothing could insult his song
which rocked in and out of his shoulder

blades   on the highway   'in the stars'
chillen   at home and abroad   weepin'

WOMB OF SPACE (YADDO)

Orb or goblet of crystal   prism
this is no kidney transplant   eat

or be eaten   the jaguar is king   food line
vertical and horizontal coupling indefinite

but not hit or miss one hemisphere is always
replete the other abundant two halves devoured

you lie back in the calm of insects still uneaten
swarms all around you yet becalmed by instincts

not fully hidden or absorbed protected haven
you stroke on your back and sides but fins pronounce

themselves near the outlet you have seen deer
other cats the anaconda of the hysterical never

eating often but fully absorbing all waters trees
open and cut bark cylinders the change of color

like the skin shedding is the art of buddhist aura
as one moves along the food chain from bottom to top

sky reflected in the water and reversible clouds
the billowing of trees sculpture made in heaven

but fired on the anvil hephaestus knew myth of return
not any circle but oracular elongated elliptical

listen to all that inhabits you watch what happens
as you move among the biosphere devouring blessing

all that lives and dies imminence of bloom shedding
you feel this at the top of the adrenals hormonal

flowering of change forgive the opposition taxed upon
fulcrums of mathematical engineering religion almanac

keeping score with the infinite inside you fully open
yet closure is separation the gift of what is always

WHAT I KNOW THIS VERY DAY

[Harry "Sweets" Edison, tribal inventor, dead at 83]

"I began in Kentucky
on a York cornet

I hated that horn
then I heard Pops

I heard Pops again
1937 I was with Count

Pres named me "Sweetiepie"
moved to L A in '50

I hated the horn
(so much practice)

when I could be playin'
with the boys

the Nation changed me
and I changed the nation"

note: Sweets's father was a Zuni Indian

ALONG CAME BETTY

for Betty Barrington

Already taken in junior high
the high fidelity of du-wahs on the avenues

gangfighting on the other side of Crenshaw
Altadena the paradise of the freeway

the future earmarked in 'trial'
John Cochran just out of LA (that's Louisiana)

Mt Vernon not Foshay
LA High not Dorsey

the fins of pisces afloat in all directions
the old world   and the new   never discussed in "Civics"

"Brown v. Bd of Education"   what's that?
Bird dead on the cutting room floor on my aunt's natal day: 3 12 55

no one   absolutely 'no one' to talk to   riding a bicycle on a Mirror route
skipped in school so one can pass the Iowa exams at 99th percentile

end up at City College
remember the issei riddles of concentration camp

play tennis on the segregated courts near USC
save Lena's son's life from white frat boys he preferred/pledging: USC trojans

wondered why Bela Lugosi's son was the best sprinter on the swim
team(now lawyer) wondered why Darryl Ellington was best sprinter in 100/
    furlong

wondered why Bill Hunter was never in shape for the quartermile
falling out at the tape for the girls he could not touch marcel or no marcel

watch George "Sparky" Anderson play second to Consolo's shortstop
weep in the rightfield clover of Rancho Cienaga American Legion fearing
    Drysdale

wondering why Edward Chapman wanted to be called "Lonnie"
wondering why Toni Harper didn't want to be called Roquelle

had stories about many buddhaheads attending sockhops at noon to
    eavesdrop
never went into the campus library until after the 'hall of fame'

wondered why no Dolphy melodies found him when he needed them most
heard Mingus and Dexter Gordon at the 54 ball room near South Park

looked forward to the All-City Relays near the Coliseum
became a lifeguard there in the deep waters of the LA Athletic Club

corpus of the Olympic team   watched Pancho Gonsalez teach any kid how
    to serve
from the dark tower: only later to learn it was Madam Walker's Harlem
    hideaway

wondered why anyone would want to leave IRT BMT Ebbets Field Polo
    Grounds Mays
finding the codes in the schemes 'off the clock' to hear Coltrane Miles MJQ

working airmail with Mingus's sister pregnant and mean deep into the
    scheme
read my WAR & PEACE in all the epics of search you could ask for in vedas

asked myself how did Betty get on the facing table making the helicopter:
    LAX
wondering how much ability 'veiled' in the Susan Miller Dorsey handbook-
    invisible

thanking her for bringing back the bad news of adolescence hormones Latin
eucalyptus senior court black prom white prom Four Freshmen Brubeck

all the things you are
when we were

well you needn't
'round midnight

Bird Lives
Nellie, My Dear

Good Morning, Heartache
"Along Came Betty"

_____

REPEAT BUTTON

_____

I usually don't indulge - Dexter Gordon
now past his 80th year - "Don't Explain"

over and over Maxine sent me this double cd
and after "Tattoo" seized me last summer

I revisit heartwork - once heartache
as a righteous sideman - on the road

when he got out of Chino - Renaissance
Club matinee on Sunset Blvd – cheering

his brim was up - still knockkneed
a grin - sweeping in from the Pacific

like the pro he was a little early
the beat as steady as his heartbeat

which had straddled generations of song
(the microsurgery of such support - at odd

hours - in the postal airmail section
where an old Mingus sat - taking names

the Watts local about to go out of service
'our people' never becoming "your people"

his attitude) - at Tivoli - maestro of Blue Note
with his brief commentary - a mastery

of our one idiom - no one could steal
"I been down so long that down don't worry me"

ever
never

DIGESTING DEXTER GORDON AT 80

Effortless vibrato in all registers
lovely speaking voice - on ballads – unassailable

[When I was green at 21 he waltzed into Sunset
Blvd Renaissance matinee - blowing glorious]

Marshall Royal had him audition for the road
left school in LA for Fort Worth – Texas

could translate everyone - 'statesman of reed'
we christened him - regular - in ensemble settings

a little behind the beat - ready to take charge - now
(loved Mr. Pork Pie Hat - even when not with Basie)

why he loved Maxine? - consult the ledger
management akin to godliness - even when over the edge

GOODBYE PORK PIE HAT

Pres's signature his moniker   the many mf's
he could verify your poetic character one trait

you brought with you into the world
(this wasn't caught on film though Dexter

had that great laugh   composite characters
is what white filmmakers see blacks   is)

yet Mingus caught Pres's stride in ballads
easing of the glottals his very song   eclipsed

in the high registers down low in Kansas City
airchecks were breathy   loved the dancers   Savoy

kept us out of there except on kitchen mechanic
'low wage' days fraternizing was bad for blood

Pres's eyebrows had this expression when Lady sang
(they didn't talk for years then one night

like old times he slipped her sultry embrace
carried her along   whatever broke them up

as pals was the best dish in Minton's pantry
both from musical families the old man strict)

how do you get people to pay attention blues
can't be captured on film   on hotel walls   takeout

it's attitude Mingus caught that poetry only
discernible in quality   once in a lifetime   pres

PHOTO: LETTER (JOEL CHANDLER HARRIS)

this has come back to me   again
postage is no guarantee   nor portage

rote is best in the table   at table
root   as in square   delicious roundwork

'never write anything down'   handwriting
an artifice   illegible   graphics

consider Beach party   for Scott & Joyce
upstairs in Paris   Scott drunk   Joyce broke

they could take up stalls in Smithsonian
from DC to the new school postcard gala

where O'Hara worked his way up at Harvard   met
Ashberry   from the moviehouse to art galleries

no place for paul laurence dunbar's elevator
but lucille clifton wrote her 'boats' for kids

first   then after six kids told the truth
she could manage dunbar couldn't   Wright Bros

buried too close to him   we must keep(niggers)
in their various places   brawn fantasy minstrels

if   when they are able to compose   and read
we can modify plantation   currency   color   money

with bright actuarial tablets   supplant white
workers   go north   get new plates   order new

money   the movies   icons   rebs again on screen
in foreign markets   bring up klan currency

that tintype of lynchee woman hanging   bridge
left there as warning   Harpes   flies won't eat

ERNESTO VICTOR ANTONUCCI

Isthmus canal channeling   33 hours labor
(obviously wanted to be born at home)

they will take your measurements
(I will speak to your soulmaking skills)

your parents are renegades   but of the city
(so banishment is not their desire   yet)

both are makers   the craft of light   say hello to Venus
(keep your eye on her   less you be woven astray   origami)

that gift   in custom assortment   must be requested
nova   snow child   butterfly   fan

the music of the world is in you
these special papers made as artforms   to praise only you

though you blossom   for your mother
though you blossom   for your father

origami (paper-folding)
kirigami (paper-cutting)

'CRAFT' TALK, *VERMONT STUDIO CENTER*

I have brought forth books
to break the seal
as solomon broke seal
with the covenant;

'fornication'
is the great truth,
fidelity is the crime,
if you are to get to heaven
on earth;
craft is an inward journey;
all around you the names
of the *saints*
are chanted in idioms,
and you must record them,
not to memorize
but to fathom
as the *Gihon* River
points toward the source;

we are in Vermont
not far from the border
and French is on the radio;
you should translate
all borders
bringing the true compass
into discussion
as transits:
Sterling Brown's **vestiges** section;
Mr. Hayden's **Paradise Valley**
adapted ballade
with many persons
anonymous
living in the margins;
let me take you through the **Mecca**
of Gwendolyn Brooks
who saved me from the pile
of contests
for I did not win;

Justice was best at syllabics
his conversation

intense as *possum*
and as southern;
the elegy is for you
in your teens
and after sixty
and you'll get there;

do not read aloud
near any piano
or the pitch
will get you;

(from then on
dark keys will resonate
in *silence*,
and you will have made space
for snow, and your umbrella):

from then on the cadences of film-noir
for your attention-span is ruined
all film in black & white & documentary
the end of structuring as in painting
the faint disclosures as in photography
your psychography of the dark room within

ELDER

You lead a small pack on a walking tour
(it has already begun to rain)

I am thinking about the word *"plangency"*
because of Bob Hayden's poem "October"

Langston's "long march" in laughter/blues
(the treeline of your spirit undiminished)

the cast "military" as *Osawatomie* packed supplies
against the *'border ruffians'* confederates

changing tunics and bedrolls to traverse
the Mason-Dixon line   and no line *honorable*

in the search for water feed   as *Douglass* cautioned
in the night-medley of his *grandma* on the next plantation

this is currency to us and so to **chapel** feints imploding
on cretonne lips   traduced in Jolson's   "Mammy"

the King of Swing losing his clarinet in '38 to Pres
and Pres satisfied to follow Lady solo too sweet to suite

even on *"Strange Fruit"*   Langston   marching to *Scottsboro*
the long hand of his journals ossified in blood and kin

I read the folder on *Brown v. Board of Education*
four *John Brown* letters in his 'own' hand

listened to the last Hughes public reading in *Lawrence*
on cassette (the parenthetical lisp as timeline *regus)

knew his racial mountain and **THE WEARY BLUES**
translated in *Cuba Libre* as only *Guillen* would sound it

commenced to "emery" board our   **'Po' Wayfaring Stranger'**
lyric from one annal to the other: public parlance/private song

*slang for *regisseur*

ON THE THEME OF SELF-KNOWLEDGE AND EDUCATION "IN SOCIETY" THOUGH NOT DEFINED BY FALSEHOODS

*"What a wonderful world of possibilities
are unfolded for the children"*
—Ralph W. Ellison on Brown v. Board of Education

"Your health is the foundation you stand on"
(he could only have meant "psychographic" health)

so I wait patiently for you to build that blessed structure as self-portrait
(synapse the wavelengths of stunning adventure ventured still)

imagination is the key to such understanding
(even Eugene Pinchback Toomer did not go far enough on race and sex)

the mirror the myth of narcissus caught in reflection
(the self is not a genie in the bottle but beloved release)

what you will make has its own resonance: the fell of truth
(betrayal is always in the eyes of the beholder BEHOLD THYSELF)

the substance of your sinews are the best testament to fulfillment
(I would place a stack of the chips on that Bingo Game hit the jackpot)

there is the comfort of sleep subterranean Scylla and Charybdis
(then true wakefulness in pleasure of kingship and one's own domain)

Shall we call it the KINGDOM OF ACTS WHERE ONLY HEROES
    TREAD
("I was a hidden treasure and I loved to be known," the poet said)

*[msh: for Patrice Cuchulain Harper when confronting all enablers of "true self-
    conscious manhood"]*

144

JOSEPH SANTOS ILETO

You were on the wrong route
(not even your regular route)

as you filled in the hot
vernaculars of Chatsworth

I assume the Filipino in you
is American

vernacular needs some comment:
it is the language we speak

so much of it not written down
a citizen parlance

of forgiving
and forgetting

who we are
as people

there are no more civic
lessons for you

I say this with deep regret
(not even knowing you)

except in the evening news
multiple blasts from a maniac

who was as regular
in his comings and goings

as you were in your route
(but he was invisible

being white and needing
serious intervention

in his disease),
a nation's terminal disorder

if we're not seriously careful
there is no forgetting

for your family
and no forgiveness

for the many patrons
who assume their mail

what was usual in first-class
delivery now 'priority'

anyone could be killed
without serious therapy

early in the natal charts
of all our kin

there are free condolences
cards NO STAMPS NECESSARY

committees and donations
from   again   the *invisible*

citizenship is very public
(so private in the daily cult

that we must intervene
even against our very families)

when they exhibit
what we know is homicidal

rage   'at the other'
we go back before the pony express

and you go back in the nation's
register of heroes

doing your job, filling in,
making our day (and night) your schedule

THE BROKE AND THE UNBROKEN

An Essay on Lawrence Francis Sykes: Citizen and Democracy, Worldwide:
   Before and After Acadème

"Strong in the broken places" your statuesque figure tells me   newk &
   trane   miles
   ahead farm security administration>
(the long frame 'of the paint' on your swollen joints and knuckles Madison
   Square Garden
   chews Howard Theatre)

The Scottsboro Boys uplifted from their chains on Guy Johnson's "John
   Henry" 'train done
   caught me on the trestle'
(Pops juryroll testimony in the one good book on the subject always in
   jeopardy
   gondolas)

Your ashes still unburied in the Jamaica Plain basement   urn more African
   than grecian
   "love the one you're with"
(what could it mean for praxis at Washington & Jefferson College in the
   median of
   coalmines at 16)

Only slightly behind him the crossroads of segregation was your Baltimore
    backyard
    chaingang to the suburbs
(allowed on Johns Hopkins campus only on Saturdays 'to clean up' yards or
    labs no
    matter)

Into the harness of Pratt Institute you became credentialed   after St.
    Louis   Dunbar   LIU
    St John's Morgan State
(those components visual framed in anarchic light it took Haiti to clearly see
    maroons
bantustans apartheid synods)

JACUZZI SERENADE

When you are halfway between Nashville
and Memphis you stop off   in Union City

Sterling Brown's "Old Lem"   waved on   outsiders
in Union City   Hayden's   "Tour 5"   was   Natchez Trace

for you   to soak you have to have something   to 'chunk'
(not far from here is a town ruled by incest

through miscegenation   is also a wooded lake
with turpentine   Chickasaw   knew this vengeance first)

so when I ask for more towels   'not to change the sheets'
there is method to such madness   Nashville   traffic

blends in with the football team   though Vanderbilt
and Fisk never met on any bridge   Chancellor's house

a way station for 'not ever meeting'   even in downtown
bookstore—SELECTED POEMS   by Mr. Hayden uncontractual

by Vanderbilt University Press   boycott   them   Confederates
retired faculty from Fisk invited in   art   collections

on low maintenance   according to assessors   faculty
living on campus   to be visited   by touring students

disallowed from parchment   loveseat   even on verandas
(plantation tradition to stay in place despite text)

magnolias   dogwood   trace   Harpes   lynching bee
inside the coat of predators   are scalps   wood alcohol

bucks unbucked   the fever of the lowdown   lower down
(such thresholds even postmaster Faulkner did not get down)

the moalt and fever of Sam Fathers at Mamie Callie's
gravestone is beyond "The Trail of Tears"   traced through "Dancing Rabbit
    Treaties"

from Jackson to Nathan Bedford Forrest's   Crossways surveyor
to see the shape of all battles   serpentine   said Shelby Foote

After Tuscaloosa I heard a rebel jocularly call me "Yankee"
as if I were from 'rhode island red'   when we fled draft riots

across the river before there was a bridge   holding forth
while walking under water   through the fields   upstream

With such high water   cartoons   are inevitable   coon
statuettes   across the brow of consciousness   inbreeding

not too far from Union City   on a lake   too close for Comfort
Inn   Hampton   where 'the wizard'   learned his lessons: MULE

ON ARRIVAL

On Arrival
no room

a fry-up
at Terminus

with bags on hold
'in the hold'

packages held with books
(mine   in it)

lounge   uncomfortable
still   no room   but upgrade

promised
at £120/night

you figure   better beds
a cd player   light   when wanted

still we wait
(days later   the bill   no upgrade)

by departure
I've left my bag in a taxi

gone to a doctor
with no street address in any guide

sick with trouble
in Liverpool station

a stone's throw   longer
to Cambridge   to Oxford

the university towns of allegiance
stress   bucolic overtones

of trainfare
and trainwar

of Isherwood's father dead in '14
him not mentioning it   ever

"Goodbye to All That"
a forest of symbols   militia-bred

our Civil War
still unresolved   confederacy

a porridge   perhaps
Hardy   Housman   Hugo   Faust

CHRISTINE FREY'S RESURRECTION

That November 5th in '02 fistula   radiation
(then stitched up   9 hours   4 surgeons)

sedated the last 12 days (intensive   3   times)
(infection   obituary   article   your   brother   Chip)

thought of you all over   UK   tour   "Halloween"
(Atlantic   777   crossover   American   with Patrice Cuchulain)

2 pubs   2 standing room-only   venue   English pounds
(so when I read to you   alone   in your true voice)

great laughter   shrunken *sphincterblush*   all over your garden
(who knew Champaign-Urbana one's whole life)

1 22 03 you passed on gracefully   no pain
(never an e-mail   but a lovely letter   fearsomely written out)

which took you days to compose   no fuss *intaglio* true
(before you delegated all things but the spirit   soledad)

which you needed to cope   exquisite *dressage*
(cope you did at even gait   under separate halter)

I brought out Mahalia Jackson's "Come Sunday" "Soul Eyes"
(by Trane & Bird's "Bird of Paradise" as your ending at *eventide*)

OPEN STUDIO

for Rachel Sousa

I conjure you(a child of paradise)
a return to the upper tresses of trees

there to restore the fallen fledgling
to the nesting position   mouth wide open   to eat

as all artists must at the high and low digestibles
of inspiration the craft of the steady visitation

to 'the work;' to find your subject   daily   as your bread
is every meal   and parliament   plateau of spices   to flavor the tongue

one can be fooled by the details of the close industry of line and space
but one intuits the silences deliberately put there

the making of force to transform all viewing
is a heavy intention   mode of seeing   mode of action

as though to still that perfect space
within you

IOWA (1961) OR *"HOW TO USE TROUBLE"* [*WRITERS WORKSHOP*]

This was no *dream* of JFK and the *movies:*
this was no "passport" for Paris (draft notice)

with Richard Wright *dead* and Sharpeville *"passbooks"* shodden
I took my "physical" in Des Moines

a woman in whites (intern) on a *revolving* stool
checking my *testes* foreskin still in *place*

(I was the same height and weight as *Jim Brown* at lacrosse
and only a few weeks later a friend of *Emlen Tunnell*

who had come to town to place all his *cash* in Irene Kinney's *apron*
the drunk he went on 'terrible' as he disappeared into Mrs. *Lemme's* shoeshine
      parlor)

Philip Roth gave me *9* units of *"C"* that first term
accused me of writing a *"pornographic"* novella   of course I did on the
      church priest

also refused to return my paper on Wm Golding's LORD OF THE FLIES
which he assumed I'd *plagiarized* (though the *'Partisan Review'*

was *stolen* from the Iowa library, same issue with *"Sonny's Blues"* in it)
I bothered not to tell *"Newark"* Phil that Baldwin was born in 1924

MSH in *1938* (a student of *Isherwood,* who'd *loaned* me his Golding *novels*
published in *England,* and the *plays* of Arnold Wesker)

Within minutes Swedish *Verne* was spread-eagle at *419 E. Washington St*
across the street from the *police station,* right next to the *'Me Too'* market

because I had spoken of *Conrad's* fable *'the nigger of the narcissus'* for real
(next I tried for a *"haircut"* right downstairs got   Inada to "move out"

when his roommates *Dick* and *Johnny*   had called him a *"Jap"*
while Lawson went out to the local market for **vittles** to prepare *'chop chop')*

Lawson had introduced me to *Vern* Rutsala in Kinney's 3.2 oasis and played
   the *jukebox*
of *'Moanin'* and *"Softly As In A Morning Sunrise"(Art* Blakey and *MJQ)*

the only *tunes* playable in the whole town: I was about to take a *bus* to the
   "Apple"
when Lawson approached: Rutsala knew Alan Pike who just left town for
   Tennessee

and knew a vacancy with pre-med Donald *Marsh* from Fort Madison
   (Parsons College
undergrad) soon we were in a *joint* 'after hours' half a chicken for a dollar

a cheating four-flusher shot in the shoulder because of a *double-dealer*
(Ms. Turkey Feathers approached and said *"I've never cooked for a poet")*

end of story of after-hours spots with a full **jukebox** in a garage *hot-house*
almost *too* close to the Missouri border (*"Border Ruffians:"* all **confederates**)

I went back to Lawson's *stories* about Levine, his *teacher* at Fresno;
how my *teacher,* Coulette, were co-editors   to *CHARACTER & CRISIS*

a **hip** anthology with Mailer's 'Superman Comes to the Supermarket'
the *Esquire* matinee fresh on the lips of Ed Skellings (daughter: *Sonnet)*

who loved to say the *magic* word drove a corvette *"Lu"* his woman
   protecting him
from Mezey's **stilletto** which I'd just taken away from him *Lamont Poetry
   Winner*

Lawson got **care** packages from home(Fresno)his record player ripping
   through *walls*
into my dining room which was a *porch* overlooking the ***police*** station

the *thump* of ***Bags*** and *'Jug'* not to mention ***Pops Bird***
   Dizzy Miles Trane Pres
the *breakmusic* after hours from the *four* corners: Moline Davenport Rock
   Island

any *raft* on the Mississippi by "Bix" we kitsched to Chicago and Detroit
then the "Drake Relays" in Des Moines with *Ramon* for Wilma Rudolph

and John Thomas   Lawson ate himself sick on *Mexican* authentic
with Ramon's people all dressed in **black**   so hot you cried as you sweated

Don Marsh's homeboys the **Harper Bros** from the same town all in *medical*
    school
and *con-men* hitting town as Iowa swept to the *Rose* Bowl   8 starters on *offense*

with *white* girlfriends wives children the *boosters* who came to town on the
    train
a *posse* I sold pennants to from a board and hawkeye *dolls* that talked and
    sang *minstrels*

the *"workshop"* was full of gossip from the *barracks* no music *3.2* beer
the competition (Lawson and MSH) the only hipsters *without* wheels for
    hectares

z(from then on matinees were *'time we paid for in advance'*)

I had run down a carfull of *rednecks* from Council Bluffs adrift in a Hillman
pulled each out of the *car* Lawson who was dressed in his own *Nehru* jacket
    sewn tight

had "busted his britches laughing" **the State Liquor Store** the only San
    Joaquin station
(then *Midland* **25**th anniversary of the Iowa Workshop Justice had a party at
    his house)

I heard the worst racist talk from Lawson's *mentor* **drunk** certainly *Shirley*
    Aldinger
Olds sedan was '*the short*' of the evening: Janet and Lawson *"Padre"* and
    Shirley

later I was to *save* Levine's life by catching him as he fell back a sack of
    potatoes
which I carried up to Chris Wiseman's *flat* above Irene "Kinney's" **bar**

the rest is history: Phil got his jaw broken(see *"SILENT IN AMERICA"*(Wesleyan)
  Mezey opened the door to *marauders* from the wrestling team *[NOT THIS PIG]*

Phil swung and 'wrestler on scholarship' kicked him in the jaw
Engle said he'd sue the Athletic Dept and Forest *Evashevski's* Rose Bowl *team*

and Phil had to go *home* with his jaw *wired* to explain to *Franny* just what happened
though I remember the *rage* of his invective against Lawson at Don Justice's *party*

Lawson too *hurt* to admit it (Janet soothed him, then they *married* and went to Durham, N.H. though actually living in Eliot, Maine where I visited a year later)

drove Shirley and *four* white girls to the **Bronx** stopping in Cleveland where all five
slept on my aunt's living room floor. *Uncle* Ernie gave me *$10* a look of astonishment

on his face for his nephew had hit the *jackpot* and Olds or no olds would *live* to regret it(later I was to read their correspondence from **Fort Huachuca** the "wizard's" *Chehaw*

riding behind a screen in the dining car all the way to **Brooklyn**: only *"A Solo Song:for Doc"* caught the nuanced poignancy *of 'sleeping car porters'* adrift on *gondolas*

Mrs. Lemme owned a **shoeshine** shop where her husband owned the whole block
and put up Count Basie and Langston when they were on the *road*: Engle told me to see

her when I arrived by *plane* on Ozark Airlines, the *mailrun*, to meet his young daughter
and *search* the blotter for *rentals* the first **African** from the west coast looking for *digs*

later *Auden* and Denise Levertov were to come to town:Engle sent me a cab(I
was with *Turkey* Feathers in Fort Madison) unafraid to drink his whiskey
or eat on the *tab grants*

he carried in his *vest* pocket but MSH was not about *to beg* read all the
theses by the river of all his predecessors: even *"The Glass Menagerie"*
which had been *rejected*

went about his business with *'friends'* in the Gold Feather Room *"Padre,*
teach me to study my outlines in the library; *Padre,* meet me at *20 W.*
Harrison, where Frank Davis

was studying for his finals with a class full of *pre-meds* in anatomy: so much
noise
Frank shot through the floor with his *.45*(they sent for the Padre:9 Prentice
St, *garage*

behind the one **black** family out near the *A&P*, took *Johnny Hodgkins* with
me, from the *windowless* hotel that smelled of cotton-candy; slept on a
hideabed when the library
closed *at 2 a.m.*

Our *landlady* lived in Des Moines and never came to collect the *rent:*
Wilma made the Drake Relays a stellar event John Thomas even cleared his
regular
height

which he'd *missed* in Rome. **Cassius** was not at the party though still chasing
Wilma
then threw his **medal** into the river in *Louisville*, Kentucky.

I should end on *Tunnell:* Larry Ferguson from Detroit wanted the
NFL "king of the varsity" knew he'd be injured if he roamed into
Emlen's 'territory' *Irene held his money*

all during the *drunk* she'd seen her husband *robbed* and herself had been
taken *hostage*

lore of why Emlen had *special* place in the Kinney *'47 all-american* hogpile
  and **capitol**

Calvin Jones and *Big* **Jim Parker** had played to a *draw* when I was in high
  school
the only time in my life I watched the *line-play* exclusively. *'Stay out of my
  territory'*

Tunnell told Larry just before the "All-Star" Game: *varsity* v. *alumni*
(downtown there was a **photo-gallery** of all the *white* varsity football jocks)

Al Hinton **#71** from Saginaw and a *painter* who lived at 20 W. Harrison
asked me if I'd ask **Oliver Jackson**, *mastercraftsman* from **St. Louis**

'would I ask *Jackson* would he *teach Al* to draw?'
we did not speak of the *"African Continuum"* in the *early* **60**'s

we went to *free* movies came alive in *"raisins" walked* the Iowa River to the
  park
fantasized the *Art* Bridge conduit of *barracks* where
    Lowell Berryman Cassill Roth

were **kings**: or were they? *Justice* certainly his *"sonnet"* on the Garden of
  Eden
a verse exercise raised to the *'fruit of the loom'* as **poetry**. Coulette's *"Intaglio"* a
  tool

BLUES AND LAUGHTER my *stolen* thesis from the library indebted to
    Langston Hughes of which I was *oblivious* having heard Auden recite
    without text: *"Sept 1,1939"*

as an undergraduate off the *"facing table to helicopter"* at the *Terminal Annex:*
facing *mail*, even the *open* stacks, piano *rehearsal* room in the Music Bldg:
    Carol Veney

who parsed *JB's* suit when he had discovered his *DREAM
    SONGS* Henry his **minstrel**
offending me as *prism* to Jolson, DW Griffith, Wilson, Jefferson, KKK, FDR,
    LBJ, JFK

the *sit-ins* were the key to raising money: *"We Shall Overcome"* sung boldly
into the *teeth* of the Young Socialist League recruiting over and under the
  veils:

THE SOULS OF BLACK FOLK, the chapter on *"The Passing of the First
  Born"*
would become *resonant* beyond all *conjuring*: another Shirley, the wrong
  "Shirley"

a *deadly* train from *Marion*, Ohio in the freezing rain deadly *viral* exit to
  Oakland
then to LA after *JOS* and Stanford and Linda *Keuhl's* research on *"Lady Day:"*

what did I know of Iowa other than *Needles*, CA where I *lost* my *'54*
  Chevie:returned
home to *"2207;"* left all records and books to my *brother*, who delivered his
  papers

the world of the *auto* with books and records:Lawson and I would have
  jumped for joy
at *bistros* near and far (even with 'small change' from selling *pennants* at
  football
games)

I was rich on books: *"Jim"* the gymnast, Cloyd *Webb* and his *woman* from
  just out of town:"*Marengo:"abortions* in *St. Louis* *"Noel"* had to monitor:
  then no babies at all.

A list of the *cavalcade*, mostly *athletes*, some *grad* school *musicians*: *"T.J.
  Anderson;"*
others *decades* before, and the *girl* who worked at the *"Turkey Factory"* after
  hours.

SHIRLEY OF LITTLE FALLS [1961, IOWA CITY, IOWA]: A PROFILE IN "INTAGLIO"

Mistress of **Little Falls** born before there was a movie "*Waterloo Bridge*"
(*left-handed* the paint of water-colors in her hair and hairy legs: off to *Paris*)

The first woman I knew who owned an *Oldsmobile* unconvertible
(our double-date at *Justice's* —the drunken rage of Philip Levine's jawbone on
    Japs)

When we danced it was to the music of Me-Too Market **Miles** "Muddy"
    Waters
(*Lawson Inada* next door his walls too thin so he moved to *Janet's* 'next door
    to you')

We slept on the floor at my relatives in *Cleveland* on E. 97th destined for the
    "*apple*"
(I drove you back and forth with ease without a ticket '& on your dance
    ticket' I pled)

The day I left   all night for *Philip Roth exam* who gave me **9 units of C for
good luck**
(I passed the lifeguard exam in *Olympic* pool of the '32 **Games** awaiting your
    arrival)

When I returned to Iowa City "late summer" nobody knew your
    "*whereabouts*"
(later I was told you were **robbed** lost everything   *shame* took you East to
    our **apple**)

I sang our song "*Baltimore Oriole*" too your curls unstraightened when we
    scrunched
(the *Iowa* Hotel across the street took reservations for one-night stands with
    regulars)

"*A Raisin in the Sun*" was all I paid for in black and white otherwise 'free
    movies night'

(I refused to hold your hand for *"We Shall Overcome"* when *Freedom Riders burned)*

McGalliard gave a make-up in the History of the English Language for my
    M.A. in L.A.
(Esquire had its summit before I came aftermath your cup-size in the paint
    of *Connie*

Hawkins and the Rose Bowl: **Lemme's** Irene Kenney's your apartment right
    next door)
(*caught* Levine like a sack on the steep stairwell even though he called Inada
    "Jap")

Then I found you on E. 18ᵗʰ St after your *affair* with a grave Chinese
    calligrapher
(when we stretched out on the floor tight *sphincters* of your Little Falls post-
    ovarian jig)

Then I met you in the *turn-style* of the **Baltimore Art Museum** a decade later
(*end-around* in line for a signed copy of IMAGES OF KIN at Morgan State
    spring
1977)

I took your *left* hand as I signed copy a photo of *"Haiti"* on the cover of
    my book
(McGalliard met me once in San Francisco at Shirley Kaufman's garden: not
    my *Shirley)*

"So where are our children"   my true **Shirley**   of the left hand *"in the paint"*
(when *we* were **robbed** that summer of **1961** I was pining for your *cameo* "in
    the paint")

The Shirley **K.** "of the garden" ran off to *Jerusalem* though she was born in
    Seattle
(then I met "Shirley" from Mt. Lake at San Pablo—in '64: **firewall** at 169 Ivy
    St.: S.F.)

The *scallions* of canvas in oils acrylics watercolors etchings oldsmobile-
    tristes
(the *etching* of your saddling in *"dressage"* were never found on you at
    Waterloo)

PHILIP ROTH

Your characters have done dark deeds
and gotten away with most of them

the Gauguin boy at the library
has not gotten away and he is not

Willie Mays which is the centerfield
you yourself cannot patrol

a zany literate frenzy at the Harvard yard
your own longrange bibliography

for all good readers know how much biography
is auto how much self how much persona

so change the gender to rhetorical truth
and put up ante to the feminist union

forgive your relatives and seminarians
at shul roshashonah yum kippur

learn to fly in the Haifa airforce
practicing your persian whose *framed tale*

is all daylight where eunuchs parade
as keepsakes to the harem

1001 nights the beloved's domain
where storyline is vespers

before the phoneline long divisions
of Judah awakened at the oasis

and you could let down your string
slight capillary to the librarian's shelf

and let that boy as character
have the books of his dreams

whose fare he could not conjure
except in his fleecelined black

imagination the surface of which is craft
at depiction, metaphor, a true image to live by

"AMERICAN MASTERS: PBS" (RALPH ELLISON)

"the hunt in books for quail"—

He wanted 'no dramatics' while alive
but you should start with the missing chapter

"Out of the Hospital, Under the Bar"
from *SOON, ONE MORNING*, edited by Herbert Hill

We asked him should it be 'in' and he said 'yes'
which is the act of reading at William & Mary

"*Juneteenth*" Bliss and *Hickman* on and off the bandstand
the Hillcrest Cemetery where "Ida" is buried without a gravestone

'can't find what you can't see, can you?'
Grinnell a shameful travesty against his honor as honorand

I could start with knowledge of Notre Dame in Indiana
(MLK Jr. right after the execution)

zealots and doctoral klan members threatening ginger colored 'mose'
as he stood on the podium in South Bend

As a child he witnessed the aftermath of the Tulsa "riot"
the cinders of "Greenwood" alive in his nostrils

took the train during Scottsboro 'trial' to Tuskegee
played his instrument studied eliotic modernism played his instrument

left,   in armed vision, while being pursued by a hands-on playful dean
took Wright to task in faerydom at Chehaw Station, the wizard's warning

explained 'equipment for living' when "Don't Explain" in a band wagonsful
knew his people had value   against truncated value   more than chattel:
    huckleberries

NEIGHBORS

Up Smith Road in North Dighton
three little children   all in a line

your mother across the street
in a bungalow   in a cabin   in a trailer

we tried to live on a cranberry *Nipmuck bog burial ground*
with iron water   making due while we rented

Highway 44   deadly commute   at odd hours
"darkroom" in a wet basement *200 year old shack*

you the local historian   two pre-school boys
baby girl no inkling of post-partum blues

like all good neighbors   passing through
we had our own problems   hyaline membrane syndrome

newcomers   interlopers   squatters
with no oldsters in any cemetery nearby

did your husband know you would drown
your daughter   have no memory of it

then kill   yourself any counselors   years
too late   after we moved away   your smudge

a trusteeship so your boys would be educated
(your husband's new wife compliant money buildup-free)

just last year the final adjustment   checks paid
the attorney cleaning up his books   paying himself

a stash of documents in three cape dockets
two judges dead   who remembers   this bad drama?

LEONARD BROWN, MUSICIAN/TEACHER

I am not used to being screamed at
in the upper register 'where Miles couldn't live'

wordsmiths are 'lovers of the seams'
fit in (on a dime) half measures are over

with one of your students   we do duets
on my crafted dramatic portraitures of players

the vocal sets all about 'phrasing'   tropes
during and after Slavery   'Now's the Time'

on "Alabama" the resonance of 4 Girls blown up
in the 16th Street Church: residence of God

on "Reverend King" the music of intentional
suffering a conscious decision to resist

oppression   "Cousin Mary"   and Trane cygnets
but making "Giant Steps"   to   "Dear Lord"

"Spiritual"   in country versions   "Juneteenth"
when fighting for freedom is   attitude   "The Promise"

the soprano Miles gave him never out of his mouth
the wild prey animal skin tenor case from Gato

"play through the pain" of any mouthpiece
"Like Sonny"   "Blue Trane" a um ni pad me um

the praxis of composition in phrasing worksongs
'to improvise' against our tradition: to sing

into the blue notes   so gracenotes   will come
in tempo   out of tempo   or no mo' tempo at all

RICHARD DAVIS'S TRAMPOLINES

Chicago, 1994

He has many;
women in small
towns make them
special
and his touch
on the balls
of the digits
give rise
to a younger man:

too happy to fall apart
in the open,
or in his office,
where he has his tramp;

he travels light,

by car when possible,
but he has his tramp,
and so close
to Chicago
where he had to walk
around Hyde Park
as a boy,
he now drives.

The program,
with Don Byron
on clarinet,
foreshadows movies;
q & a features
the best he knows;

well, Gunther
Said Sassy
had the best pipes
in this century;
this isn't Gunther's
idiom, on this campus
or any other

but Mr. Bassman
goes on to say
he toured
5 1/2 years with St.
"Divine," then moves
to another question,
emanations off the beat
in "Mr. P.C."
Trane's tune for
Paul Laurence Dunbar Chambers:

both men avoided
pimps, gangsters, dressage,
getting to practice,

and being beat up
while protecting
their instruments:

he would die for it
getting to Miles
so modalities
would register
in half-measures.

Byron, who hates
the middle-class,
greets fusion
as styles/alloys;

he was told
he could never
master the classics,
his narrow lips
too thick
for modulations;

grads and undergrads
twittered:
Davis, who was late
to work,
had to get home
to Madison
to tune up;

the rest went to dinner
off Michigan Avenue;
we got paid;
for an extra day
I went out of the neighborhood,
got towed
from an all-night
foodlot,

retrieved my rental
in the snow;

Richard knew better
than to stay:
"Billie's Bounce,"
"Off minor,"
"Scrapple from the Apple,"
the best place to be:

Scarface, with "Fatha"
Hines playing only
the black keys
paid top dollar
if he liked you;

this seminar'
with vertical theory/
horizontal living proof
is aerobically over: thanks to Richard.

_____

YEAR OF THE FIREPIG IN CHINESE NEW YEAR

_____

Seven years back I lost a friend who died at home but ate no pig
(he was no muslim and no "firehorse" and he loved to cook)

Today we have leg of lamb in the oven in his honor to heal his bruises
(his son and namesake has his own "blues" over these seven years also)

A girl sat at his table holidays 'big-legged women with manners was his
    downfall'
(he extracted a promise from his physician-wife to provide exit-pills at his
    end)

I saw his daughters from that marriage 'go blank' at busstops near Brown's campus

(others who loved him his mother first murdered by a 'salesman' in her own home)

The Chinese in Chinatown in my favorite city eat FirePig in their own family restaurants

(I knew a Mei-Mei and Mei-Ling and Yin-Yin as a boy in Fillmore supple as ginger)

Later to breathe all night at Permanente Kaiser through E. Coli 'neonatology' cell

('the enemies of promise' everywhere fomenting eugenics in W. S. where all get eaten)

The second wife withheld the pills to ease my friend's last breaths

(a Hippocratic oath or a Jamaican rubirosa cigar an island getaway fully furnished)

This is all in code for I was born in the year of the Tiger lost my neighborhood 'duplex'

(never recovered from the deceit of the beloved and watched men fail warned or not)

The Pig is one thing but the FirePig once every sixty years is "Beauty Shell" covenant

(a lifetime of dread the spit open [NOT THIS PIG] upside down, eyes open)

Sing Sing and Treasure Island full of lifers 'dead in the hole'—then let out to kill

(mandarin writings "Message from the Nile" sphinx all at high table FirePig)

EULOGY FRAMED AS REQUIEM MASS
ON THE AMERICAN FRONTIER

You will be best known for the music of "Shaft"
which you were given many times across the prairie

On the trains later organized by Sleeping Car Porters
you took such news as travel as commentary on Art

Yours was the embracing of self as artifact your rough
exterior culled mustache elan vital true fashion statement

LIFE was just an exercise Brazil a continent apart poverty
a sore point on the ethos of exploiting the 'body and soul'

musicians caught so you wrote that down that music
then asked to be buried where your mother waits for you

We will play your music across the disciplines: high modes deluxe
American Vernacular Free Expression Unshackled Brown Baby Boy

MODULATIONS ON A THEME . . . FOR JOSEPHUS LONG

Not far from Harvard Square
between New Year's and Xmas
we file into the sanctity
of your name: Josephus Long,
long on the details
of nuance and residue.

I met you in the winter
of 1964, in the snow

of Wiltwyck School for Boys,
in Esopus, New York;
you'd commute to New Paltz
at odd hours
counseling your charges,
boys 8–14,
who craved the structure
and elegance of your laugh,
but could not hear the perfidy.

At basketball you were silk,
sometimes brought down by brute
power, the elbows of equality
you would not stomach
as you swept for the goal;

your bright, black face
was like the best Brazilian
coffee, without cream,
and so creamy women
came to your doorstep
with all they had to give,
an estuary aflutter,
an estuary forsaken
on the remnants of the Hudson River.

And so we came to Bard
and Vassar for the scent,
and the scent came;
though the girls came for crafts
to teach to children,
their wombs spoke differently
and so we had to speak of solace,
and how to resist the symbolism
of flesh, ours and their own:
we swam on those rivers,
were instructed by the suckholes

and rapids of a shallow river,
ran our tongues over placenames
still forbidden, and anchored
in the speech of Coltrane,
who talked exclusively in song.

Driving on the Taconic
in the blue-dark of spray,
and fearing oncoming traffic,
we headed for the "Half-Note,"
after work to catch the last sessions.

You were awed by Elvin,
McCoy was young, aesthetic,
almost your age, and Jimmy,
Jimmy was learning to play
in the steam of subway cars—
and Coltrane came.

No need for sleep!
We checked, in team meetings,
the virtue of enrichment,
sacred period of custodial
control, when we could get the kids
to write letters;
and there were the tailors,
exclusive domain of local women,
who sat like cranes in the buzzard's
roost of the administration building,
but they were white,
unafraid of black/hispanic
mafia kids,
more afraid of Mennonites
who ran errands everywhere,
and what they said
counted in more than needles and thread.

They lived for character,
and from where they sat,

they saw everything:
you would bring your charges
into the courtyard
in a straight line,
in clean clothes,
ready for the routine
of the 600 School Review—
600 schools were remedial schools—
and so when the herring ran
we would have runaways;
we had runaways on good days
and on bad;
we would report to the shrinks
and the social workers
what little we knew of design,
for in the files, the psychiatric
files we were not supposed to read,
we found the answers,
cost commentary on the underclass,
the vacuums and votive candles
of the future
for they were sacrificial lambs.

Still, we fought for them,
and when we drove to Grand Central
into the general population,
all their canteen money
as carfare home,
we wept for them,
but we wept secretly:
we had put them to bed,
soothed their nightmares,
retrieved them from the runaway
streams, fed them with pointless
forks, bathed in predatory
sores, patched them up with needle,

thread, and the buttons
of timeless assault,
our institutional homeland.

We did not speak of *bantustans*,
for this was before the jargon
of oppression,
we spoke of a chance;
the girls from Bard and Vassar,
they brought their softness,
and the shrinks met monthly,
with reports on the reserves.

We live by analogy:
I told you to keep your hands off
of what you couldn't support
for a lifetime;
these are the seeds of love.
We drank *Antiquary* scotch
from an Irish stream
in Catskill, New York
where my father was born—
I pointed out the Day Line
where my grandfather worked,
how he lost his eye
to a pop bottle
that blew up in his face;
how he *made* the sweet strings
and palate of the mandolin,
and wouldn't let his wife
work, for anything,
took pride in being 'the only one'
in town, took pride in *battle royales*
for spending money to feed his family.

And so we battled on the riverways
in Rome. New York, where you were born,

and where my uncle traipsed on
Griffiss Air Force Base—
lost his life driving friends to Utica.

So when I heard the mortifying
word, carcinoma,
I came to attention
as a coach runs ascant
to a star running back,
or shortstop, or to the tennis
net where you laid out your habit
in celestial whites,
for you were ruthless at the net,
and in the forecourt,
and your serve was coming around
into the corporate empires
of the inner sanctum:
now there was time for: fun.

You had the faith of your mother, Eva;
you had the intuition of Alex, your father,
who sits in his Town Car
waiting for dialysis,
which is the sight of your face
in the speedlane of the Thruway
coming home; home is your sister,
Rosalyn; it is the beauty of children
at play where all pulled their punches;
all played by the ubiquitous rules.

Deception in your brilliant facades,
and in the mechanics of cooptation,
you met your match in *New Mexico,*
spirit center of the Navajo,
the high winds of andeluvial change,
and her fealty was the law

and how to count
even your foibles
and property gain.

The salon opens into the magical sound
of a sunroof in the stars
as a shield is made from Orion,
from Big Bear, from Asia Minor.

EVA'S SONG AT THE END

PSALM
Strange
that a harp
of a thousand
strings
should stay
in tune
so long

Roses you cast fitfully over your son's grave
in Cambridge
(an image I refuse to forget
as you refused the extreme unction
as penance
to a life well-lived)

you were my aunt's best friend
when she had no kin to rescue her
after her husband died on River Rd
in a foursome crash
no one could explain

run off the road perhaps
but not at home with his wife
the twisted wire of communication's men
roped off at Griffiss Air Force Base

as you held court nearby
to all souls and bodies spent and broken
as vestibule to the tabernacle:
"every time I hear the spirit in my heart I will pray"
the only rehearsal you could never make
as pilgrimage to Delta Lake
where I almost drowned as a boy

I saw your skin refuse to wrinkle
(smooth as silk)
Alex in his parked town car he could no longer drive to town
(the town Rome, New York a northern levee before the '27 flood of Bessie
    Smith)

"my house fell down and I can't live there no more"
refrain to take the chains off men and women in bondage still
I saw you give the petals of a full life freely given to all
"the CHANT OF SAINTS wasted on the lost and found

while you resisted every token of blame
(I watched you dance with my father in ceremonial calm)
the thought of Michael in the garden with your walker
a new blanket of oxygen for him to live
a ballad of remembrance this final ditty
the mercy of the savior finally come for you

the mercy of the savior finally come for you

LOS ANGELES COLISEUM OLYMPIC
SWIMMING POOL, 1960

You sit in your perch, 6-12/2-6,
as the swimmers do their regimen,
eight lanes or nine
is the superstition
of the coaches, the handlers
setting the pitch
for all strokes;
and the relays
are extra,
the light smell of chlorine
vectored into body lotion,
caps
and the ubiquitous swirl
of the kick
which hunts in cycles
as a shark
underwater.

With goggles, a long poll,
and uneven fins
you brush the deep end
early
so the sediment
callows
to the drains;
at seventeen feet
your eardrums pop,
only a jockstrap
to recoil
the best upperbody
workout

in the ghetto
which is where you live
according to the white-haired
superintendent
of city water,
in-service training,
and the wisdom of race rituals
he tells as jokes
to amuse the lifeguards:

one such joke
is about the bulletheaded
"blackboy" who would not stop
running to the whistle,
and once fell off the three
meter board,
losing his balance on a cutaway,
and gibbon-like
grabbed the edge
of the rocking board
and fell askew
to hit his head on the deck,
the diamond patterns of the edge
like a razorback:

the bullethead boy
would walk away with a welt
and not like the pits
of a splat watermelon
in a 1930's movie skit
and so be vectored
into the humor of the sup
and all the nervous
inductees,
including the bouncer,
rotund, on the payroll,
and black as the enforcer

to lifesaving techniques
in the deep end.

Meanwhile, it is Saturday,
and *Pancho* is teaching all
kids on the tennis court
to serve; I learn his techniques
from this distance
as I patrol the lanes
of the swimmers,
on this day the girls
Athletic League team
who are girls
entering pubescence,
their scales
glistening in calories
they shed
in intermural meets
with the boys
who challenge them
to lower the clock
and shed their onepiece
suits for the cream.

One retrieves a dummy
in seventeen feet,
crosscarries the burlap
sack to the edge,
hoists oneself
and the dummy
out of water
and assumes the position
to resuscitate;

for live action
the bouncer allows
you to drift to the bottom,

as a diver would
from the platform
(not so fast)
and grab you from behind
so you might use your techniques
in the mimeoed skit
and bring him to the surface,
to the edge,
hoist him out:
assume the position:

FREDERICK ARMSTRONG HETZEL

(Obituary as exegesis, on the death of my first publisher)

You tracked me down to announce   my nomination(in poetry)
for the National Book Award (1970)
a book you did not want to publish   nor keep in print
the judges Warren Levertov Brooks   could not agree
I did not win the contest (Wesleyan had already said
"we have our black book")   but Gwendolyn wrote me
on her immaculate peach paper   "YOU WERE MY CLEAR WINNER"
so I told my mother   who'd put the letter in the freezer
"let's wait a day or two to see if there is more to this story"
and your telegram came from Pittsburgh(I thought of Josh Gibson)
later we changed the title from BLACK SPRING
to "Dear John, Dear Coltrane"   a poem I could not publish
anywhere   I went back to my classes   ending the book for a Biafran
Odinachi Nwasu   who had not heard from his family   in Nigeria
'another brother gone' was the refrain   "Biafra Blues"
Achebe was to ask me later   when I was at Providence Plantations

182

where did I get the idea   a student   I answered the poem
found its home in *Okike* while "Dear John..." remained unpublished
a bad omen for a book whose title poem remained unpublished
"too sentimental"   then Stephen A. Henderson asked me the query
"was the first line a reference to Sam Hose who fought back
after being assaulted on his master's farm"   that Du Bois

had returned home to protect his family during the Atlanta riot
his derringer loaded   his family hidden in the stairwell

was that the Sam Hose I alluded to   his fingers and toes meat
displayed on Peachtree   was that the church that answered

each question with the same answer   the only answer to violation
"a love supreme"
(I had no telephone during the January thaw in Minnesota but walked by
snowshoe across to the point   upwind   across
a frozen lake   in Kandiyohi County   up a path to a country
phone)   my book was one of nine   you were happy   after pause

you said "Michael, we're so proud to have published your book"
and I said 'it won't win; but thanks for calling.'   Out of Print!

ZAMBIA

---

for Frank Chipasula

What did I know of detention
after a few hours in Protea Station
jail?   I was there for a few hours,
they took my briefcase full of poems,
told me I was there without a permit,
reminded me I was a guest of the govt,
their govt; *my Afrikaans was poor.*

I could only make out the fist of each
interrogator, one like Stewart Granger,
one like Tom Mix, *in my cinema childhood.*

Listen to me: all the chiefs have beads
that sing in the palate; ***the children
of Morris-Isaacson school have told me so:***
they peered through the   blackboards—
I said through the blackboards—
as I chanted the lullaby "a love supreme"
about the great magician, John Coltrane;

***his story was their story, and in two lines
they were chanting with me.***

*As I left the campus they were at the screens
like locusts on barbed wired,
jeering the hippos, which patrol their alleys;*

***I will not call them streets;
I will not call them roads.***

So I came to you at the installation
from prison; I had been captured on video
and on television—***American officials
asked me to stand still on versions of the story.***

*I had stood still at Evaton, where my great
grandfather bought the land, freehold land,
for Fanny Coppin Hall, a women's residency
at Wilberforce Institute; the cornerstone
reads 1908, so I read to the children
of Evaton at the cornerstone
and I was smiling the broad smile
of Azania:* **"Nkosi Sikelel' i Afrika,"**

*as God blessed Bishop Johnson's flock
as he moved about on maneuvers;
once a python crawled across him in the bush,*

the jacket of the great snake abandoned to him;
now we are embattled in another chimera of skin.

Listen to me; I know there are lakes in every dream
you conjure, that you miss home, your broken
vertabrae and pustule alive on detention's throne;
we must not say this is an evil throne;
we know it is not the golden stool;
for this symbolism many countries have died
unnatural deaths—we will make a new word for prison.

MASSEY'S MINISTRY

"I have done the state some service
  and they know it."
—*Othello*

"A whale would sell for thirty times
  what you would, **Pip,** in Alabama."
—*Moby Dick*

"Rich man Dives he lived so well, don't you see
Rich man Dives lived so well, don't you see
Rich man Dives lived so well
When he died he found a home in hell
He had a home in that Rock, don't you see.
Po' boy Lazarus, po' as I, don't you see
Po' boy Lazarus, po' as I, don't you see
Po' boy Lazarus, po' as I,
When he died he found a home on high
I got a home in that Rock, don't you see."
—(spiritual)

Nine muses for the **nine** presidents
who must—on deferred maintenance—

negotiate our structures of change—
zygotes (certainly), metaspace, and scripture:

"I don't know why my mother wants to stay here fuh;
this ole worl' aint be'n no friend to huh."

"Been down so long that down don't worry my—"
    (been down so long that down don't worry me)

near the year 2000, not yet doublefault,
doubletreed: a heart with a brain unsutured

by poker, in pokerface, ashrined in tuxedo,
and on the internet, physics as unseen

patterns of spring training: **John Hope**
writing his own *pass* to slip by

illiterate confederates, the flag still flying.
                    Even in Hattiesburg

you were taught to bind up the nation's wounds
and overcome homesickness

by journeying inwardly—no forty acres or a mule—
to stand on the levee
at crest stage in St. Louis (Twain country for sure)
listening to neighbors upstream

scream obscenities to the inner city
held in a flood, "to stay home,"

in fear of exodus and revenge
after causing all this trouble

with buzzard's roost
near the 'gateway of the west.'

Johannesburg, the hippos
on patrol, have camouflaged President

Mandela's wintry cabinet
as you have sought protection in

Bengamin Mays's earliest childhood memory
of riot, his good books

now loam to defrost the *Upas* tree
of the Family of Man

in Atlanta,
      so on your rounds consider Reverend
King's *intentional suffering*
          as moral art to all curricula.

Do not fear the metaphysical highway
nor the exegetical ether—

you can't run home to mama—
student E-mail offerings

strategic on the Internet, Angels
awake, off-hours, from highway to cowpath.

Cows continue to come home
in the nation's long dialogue—

it is a speech vernacular
even before the founders,

freedom movements,
          continuous acts inside

your heart. It is a style
of real values beneath your idiom:

it is the physics of "*The Mecca*"
housing project . . . 'in my father's house

there are many mansions,'

                              perfection in the act.
So minister to a circuitry
of great ideals in the real world;
abide commitments to democracy
on every presidential day(and night)

This is more than one technologist's dream:
remember no fixed limits

or capacities of any individual
human being, even in this wren's nest,

more than grid, garden, or map:
this ministry is an ideal:

not a political system,
certainly not an actual state of pedigree

we will configure a new menagerie;
we will surrender to *Massey's* ministry.

Muses: nine beautiful
daughters of Zeus, who
inspire literature, science
and the arts. Each had her
particular field of activity:
Calliope, epic poetry; Clio,
history; Erato, love poetry;
Euterpe, lyric poetry in
general; Melpomene, tragedy;
Polyhymnia, sacred poetry;
Terpsichore, choral song and
dance; Thalia, comedy and
idyllic poetry; Urania,
astronomy.

Presidents of Morehouse College:

Joseph T. Robert	1884–1885
Samuel Graves	1885–1890
George Sale	1890–1906
John Hope	1906–1931
Samuel H. Archer	1931–1938
Benjamin E. Mays	1940–1967
Hugh M. Gloster	1967–1987
Leroy Keith Jr.	1987–1994
Walter E. Massey	1995–2007

THE TANK AND ITS NARRATORS

Saturdays in the dank hallway of **Horace Mann:**
in the mailbox are letters needing to be read;
those that need to be written float
near the waste basket—it nearly empty.

Who is your tailor when it comes to jeans?
no doubt a memory of Flatbush Avenue,
along with the memory of Lincoln
in his habit of serving out
the nation's morality
in lessons of the couplet
if morality is expediency
with a punch.
            Wit for **Nick**
is great patience with the witless,
and strange demeanor at meetings
when one leaves early to a straw vote,
few issues worth a late meal
or a phone call from a foreign publisher
whose accent is incredible
on the flashboard of AT&T.

Germany is sometimes uncomfortable,
at "Checkpoint Charlie"—the Berlin Wall
of 'intentional suffering'—when Dr. King was torn asunder—
even with the sacristy at Rhine River;
like Thomas Mann you brood over the psalms
of the individual
with comments on *children*
who make you proud
or whom you fail:
this cultivates a healthy
restraint for straight religion.

One seldom appreciates the vapor
of every 19th century man;
it is the wit that stings
with a tooled resonance
for stark reversals:
it is more than man vs. the machine
though anyone can copy the cadence
of *John Henry,*
his iron platform, the mountain,
his game pulpit voice:

this is the choir of Juneteenth:

it is the shadow that Father Abraham
forced his wife to look
into at the dead center of the asylum
after their favorite son
had died a terrible death.

IT IS THIS LOVE OF SHADOW
that makes you stand on good legs
under *the Emancipation Tree*
on the HAMPTON, VIRGINIA campus:

the events of the tree are strangely simple
leaving much unsaid, a flowing tank of water
attached from a *fountain,* the tank far from empty.

JUDGE & JURY: A SAGA ON DRAMATICS OF THE PERSONA
OFF STAGE

for George Houston Bass, 1938–1990, in memoriam

Because he had aversions to mass-produced
tailors he was caught on needle and thread;

After the closure of the cervix there were stars
on his planet, for he talked to children inside him;

Because the A.M.E. Church archives should have been
manageable in Nashville but went up in smoke in Philadelphia garages;

After he stood on the Ganges he could out of the body
trip in exasperation for deadlines, straight-no-chasers;

Because "Juneteenth" was a scriptural holiday
with white/black, black/black ministers calling our names;

After "Garvey Lives" raisins in the sun had to make copy
on the traditional time-zone of a capella brushwork, cymbals;

Because ashes need rugs for full display,
dancing on heads of pins in the cobra/mongoose amphora;

After the "striptease of reality" clause
in the contract ritualized on Providential Plantations;

Because Langston was barred from Saratoga Springs
waterholes without a note from Mrs. Ames;

After she wrote a forced march to *HUAC*
with footnotes on workhabits, haberdasher, 20th Century Ltd;

Because the artist as a maker <u>makes</u> "force"
we stand entrapped in the magic circle of the mode;

After the environment of the mode
enchants all who live in the life-force effort;

Because you did not defer
we ambled up crystal stoups, train-trestles, microsoft;

After the documents were signed/sealed/delivered
we torched the contract-wheel, "out of nowhere," <u>confirmation.</u>

THE REVOLUTIONARY GARDEN

> *How shall the mind keep warm*
> *save at spectral*
> *fires—how thrive but by the light*
> *of paradox?*
> —Robert Hayden

Hieroglyphics of the mace,
the posture of the faculty,
pose of building and trustee,
janitors come and gone:
the service industry of the deep night
now gatekeepers of deep mines,
facile libraries,
a prominent Abraham Lincoln,
apt phrasing, personal losses,
his mad midwifery of the nation's
cylindrical wounds
of the black feminine persona,
a mindset of **Sojourner Truth.**

She is suspicious of speech on the run,
the pastel banners crisscrossed
in the oleander lights of the public
square, the flexible fire-escape.

The human rite in secret blood
and sinew, the science of defensive
starting phrasing, the idol labs,
their great dorsal fins of circuitry
blooming everywhere,
the not so pure products of America

needs a balancing act on the wintry trapeze,
bigger than *Chaplin*, more special
than wavering tongues and herringbone,
the necklace of divinity:
we sit down on our prayer rugs
and ubiquitous tea,
in the fuse and muster of the constable
for her heart listens all your life:
she does not sleep on the expedient wishes
of the few, remembering
the child alive in the man,
kissing the direct, crucible in the ark;
this revolutionary garden.

ROYCE HALL

[Ellington's Muse on Centennary of His Birth, with special
thanks to Kenny Burrell, master guitarist from Detroit, who
put this tribute to EKE together despite 'trained incapacity'
and "entrainment" at UCLA campus]

Coltrane played here; Miles, never!
too many historians make light of *segregation*

not understanding denotative geography,
understanding nothing of the hurt

especially in music:
Ellington's forgiveness shant be forgot

we dance into the passing lanes of
Charlie Barnett, Jimmy Lunceford

both playing to the Indians, encamped,
Cherokee, Chickasaw Stomp, or was it jump

[my love has my tickets to the fare
a doctor in the making the other

cousins on both side of the Panama Canal
no one but **Milt Jackson** indispensable]

she will learn 'all the things you are'
in little more than a fortnight

fondling the Spanish text of my affections
in the lexicon of code, and codes broken

for she is *double-agent* to postmodern kin
where kinship ties foresake and are foresaken

yet music is every part of her idiom(**Ivie A.**)
quick movements of the dance forever latin

the tango glistening in workout stations
of the rich and poor in *democratic* steps

she can lock into whenever she chooses
the *Padre* disguising little she can't feel

GWENDOLYNIAN STACCATO DANCE

---

you were difficult to read by phone
reachable by postcard mostly from *Yaddo*

your natal day right after my sister's
my chores set out in the idiom of embrace

as only those who craft words for one's betters
can know the straightjacket of an open field

even from this den with range and perch
your cadences are broad and deep Montreal abides

as another province in another country
yet you are French-Canadian in attitude *svelte*

in the *borderzones* of peninsulas St Lawrence
the quadrant of a corner you depicted photograph

in the report of generations why *hwy* 61 blues
inadequate to your parsed blueprints *blueblack*

the umbrella of color arched in stockyards
elevators trestles the pawnshop man in watches

reports in the Defender of every flight galore
when one is under siege less is always more

budget for the many ribbons in your hair
a curling iron and the straight pomades

of *oilchange* and *oilfilter*   Army brigands on let
would load the docks and dock themselves dozens

the woeful number on short shrift chains
a *rooming house* closet of books   *your passion fruit*

strings of pearls the rhyming lexicon pause
in stunning recognition of your perennial box set

MUSE

On the porch of the secret stairway
a *bee hive*

I watch the coming and going
near the statue of Brutus

as metaphor to Union Avenue
when Lincoln bound up the Nation's wounds

Yo-Yo Ma was about performance;
he sang on the cello

to novices and journeymen alike
forgetting the late hours of his perfect pitch

turned inward for an exacting father
and gave all who asked and did not ask

and moved on into the layered zones
of music carried within

a magical ignition
he could touch even when empty

a bowl refracting in the air
and Lincoln's words were his own (mostly)

Brutus an ancient patrician
who did not know how to protect himself

Toomer's beehive a trope on slavery's
violation of the dark beauty of women

and you have come to me to heal
with no profit I can see but the good

of the hive   her hope and honeycomb
alive in the free gift   *and she was sweet*

SPENCER TRASK'S DEN (YADDO)

This is the master's lair,
his modest perch, on all sides,
eclipsed in trees,
downwind the rose garden
"For Katrina's Dial"
the true words of confederates
on Union Avenue:

Brutus is here, Falstaff,
the brass bed and oversize
tub a steerage of the mind
at play in the market
where *railroads*
are grids over homelands:

indigenes starve;
they gather pollen,
flies flock (when the horses
leave) in stalls;

I did not photograph
Virginia normal schools
in the 'uplift;'

views on lynching were firm
and I have persisted
in what I see at the firm;
considerate patronage/
malign neglect.

In this age you build
an outpost of progress;

in this world (as in the next):
Katrina's handiwork
in the children
for the children's children:

freight, and coinage for freight,
for bondsman; for steerage.

SPOON OF WMM III: LOST REFLECTIONS
ON MY IPOD NO LONGER SHUFFLING

—for Lieutenant Commander William Morris Meredith,
1919–2007, in memoriam

Que Negro Esta[ITALUBA]
Prescription for the Blues[HORACE SILVER]

Spartacus Love Theme[BILL EVANS]
Eye of the Hurricane[HERBIE HANCOCK]
Close to You[GEORGE DUKE]
Little Madimba[McCOY TYNER]
April in Paris[BIRD]
Alabama[JOHN COLTRANE]
High Modes[HANK MOBLEY]
Come Back Interlude[JANET JACKSON]
Off the Wall[MICHAEL JACKSON]
The Hard Blues[JULIUS HEMPHILL]
Django[MILT JACKSON]
Tivoli[DEXTER GORDON]
"Deep Song"[GAYL JONES, his best student sent to me for safe harbor, her
    own crew]

Today is April 14th OR any depth 2007 a Saturday while we are at watch for
    the crew
(when you were *three* he gave you his spoon: and William Meredith ate by it)

Do you have that spoon? You will need it for more than porridge homegrown
(I fed you applesauce on the shoulders of Hwy 23, RR1 56273 with that
    spoon)

My iPod is full of Duke Ellington and Coleman Hawkins Pres & Lady Day
(I pottytrained you in one weekend in my parents house at 2207: 213 931
    6400)

I fed you near campus in air-conditioning in Tuscaloosa "Alabama"
    bivouacked
(you left your lunch at 15 over a long weekend caught between East & West
    H.S.)

Meredith wrote an elegy for W. H. Auden [silver spoon] **EFFORT AT
    SPEECH**
(the title his poem for Muriel Rukeyser who parsed 'the Amistad' for Mr.
    Hayden)

You asked in my office with no spoon handy 'what did I think of your
    writing'?

(I said you had "aptitude" that could not be taught—-you called me '*Nasty*'
   again)

And so you "lied" to me steadily into your 36th year "text-messaging"
   spoonless
("lying's not death do not grieve" said "Pa" Hayden caught in Crystal Cave
   elegy)

On this day a decade ago I sent you to Paris: "Man is a social animal" said
   Zain Afa (**Kumar**: 75109: youngest of seven from Egypt: why you studied
   Arabic at Pasadena)

City College where I student-taught under William Trevor, September 1964:
   spun:
(*William Morris Meredith III* – **Nelly Keyser**: collateral descendant: WMM,
   sec. of)

Treasury, under Pres. Zachary Taylor: before WMM had a *stroke* in '83,
   fought
(*expressive aphasia*: **Trees, students and poetry were the three loves of his
   life**")

Do not forget his *silver spoon* given to you in utmost love before you could
   talk.
(You left your toys in truss in Meredith's *Bread Loaf*, Vermont cabin
   commode.)

Dulcie M. Scott, from Cleveland, Ohio, gave me the "bill" from her
   plumber:
(watery black fly also meant "*The Wreck of the Thresher*" in 1963)

An American atomic *submarine* that sank off Cape Cod: 129 crewmen lost.
(compare his poem to my "RHODE ISLAND (SSBNT740): A Toast"
   written)

"—*For the Christening of the USS Rhode Island and its crew*" and not quite
(good enough to dedicate its compost to Meredith's spoon given his way to
   you)

"Speech just began to return to me" after long years of his own "therapy and
    travel,"
(*Lieutenant Commander William Meredith* spoke duly to 'trees, students,
    poetry')

when he was laid to rest in Bala Cynwyd, PA. family cemetery: "study his
    spoon"
('someone you would like to know better may not feel the same way'—
    beloved)

his ashes bled into the very lives his good works shined as escort in "war &
    peace"
(like *Tuskegee* airmen on the wing he never lost you:
    his "**trees students poetry**")

"NEWK" WHILE HE'S STILL ALIVE AND PLAYING

Imagine this: Ralph Ellison, master novelist and 'king of phrasing up close,'
    "antagonistic cooperation"
(boycotted at N.Y.U. for all ten years as Albert Schweitzer Professor of
    Humanities)

by the agents of Imamu Amiri Baraka a.k.a. LeRoi Jones from
    Newark   Ralph examined Amritjit Singh's   thesis
(town of Newark begat Sassy & Wayne Shorter   in service to
    Pres Trane "like Sonny" the poets of   phrasing with range)

I taught at NYU as "Berg" Professor in 1992 with a WSV #12H apt
    overlooking Bobst Library
(I taught Tuesday evenings from 7–10 at 19 University Place to all-
    comers living and dead)

the culture of the class was hanging out after class over pitchers at the
    nearest corner bar recasting the   unsaid
(I put an end to these "silences" after two meetings the
    recasting bad commentary in stupor to lost   sleep)

I had conferences   to recommend "teachers" after five weeks of class   and
    no files
(this was psychodrama of a very high pitch one on one with no praxis   but
    highly competitive for jobs)

so one day in class the babe from Brooklyn with the 7 year old girl didn't
    show up Mengele obsessed
(I told this 'long-poem obsessed' mother to bring the child to class we'd
    cope and she did   invented   titles on the spot for Newk)

"The Bridge" was first and there were others for two weeks she didn't ask a
    thing her live-in the expert   afraid
(I told her a recording a tune for the Brooklyn Bridge   left it at
    that write it soon Mengele or no   mengele)

the cast of characters played out despite the beer two black women one gay
    from Jersey one confused   from Chicago
(others wending their wintry ways to
    "publication" contests stylistic cvs   but no reading
    lists   nothing   on reserve at Bobst)

they wanted another class for the Berg apt but the boss had missed a
    deadline to file I gave a lecture   instead 7 year old came with
    mama
(I layed out a few notes on tradition black and white in between across the
    arts modernism ashcan   school painting prosody)

I made the secretary of the program black a poet from Queens say she was
    proud my reading list   layered out in Bobst 8th circuit
(asked me if I'd met Baraka   his progeny   I kept time with   visits to
    named classrooms of Ellison,   James Weldon, Woodruff)

I did one contest as judge without pay   choosing my own
    screener   paid to read the same pile I read   myself

(an outsider from Kansas won   took my father to the Schomburg where
    "the family archives" shone   after many boxes)

Anonymously I called on the woman assigned the Bridge and she came
    forth with an original poem   Newk's ambition fulfilled
(the child grew up Mengele died in South America again and again the girl
    from Chicago middle class   from Yale gave up overalls)

We will all grow up in the library if we're asked to made to supply our own
    archives for the children
(Newk knew this with his many practices on "The Bridge" too free to jump
    off into anything   but the   grace of tradition)

I have a special place   heart for my neighborhood   in B'klyn P.S. 25 the
    nits   jollystompers   Eastern Parkway BMT Cypress Hills
(born in the same house as my mother delivered by the same man best
    friend of Schomburg 'let me get   my papers' for Newk)

HORACESCOPE

In 1958
      over Xmas
         with my own tux
            I was given
"Six Pieces of Silver"
        as a gift
          from my host's
            mother: Miriam Johnson;
I was on leave
      from the terminal annex
         L.A.P.O.
           for three weeks;

my first encounter,
                in the Bronx,
                                was to be mistaken
in my Botany 500
                as *Floyd Patterson*
                        all heavyweights
                                  in shape
looking very much
                alike;
                      went to dance
                            to *Machito*
                                  at Roseland;
not allowed
            to dance
                with any
                      of the *Puerto Rican*
                            women;
I was in company,
                with the headhunting
                            lawyer: Norman Johnson;
                            at a benefit
                                  for killers;
still,
    could not
            touch
                their women
                      even
                        with space
                            between us;

then I went to see *Horace Silver* at the *Five Spot;*

his wig was wet with sweat, completely unprocessed,
and flowing; put those Puerto Rican women to shame,
arthritic rhythms of *Cape Verde* in his feet and fingers;

obviously spawned in the black church of the village veld
off the coast of **Africa**, and the *Mayflower* Hotel.

I was 20; that was 50 years ago; the fresh squeeze
of "*Señor Blues*" is upon me, even in the lyrics
with Bill Henderson crooning, in salt & pepper,
to any takers, male/female/black/white: slip into the breaks
to get one's complete **horoscope**, on and off the ivories.

MILES DAVIS SHIRT: MONTERREY JAZZ FESTIVAL

Your image in abundance
the b flat finger hushing us

who wrap up our *beloveds*
in a hang tail overtone

of melodies only you could compose
much less play

in the body only such resonance
of a tee shirt   on sale

in the enterprising zone
of entrepreneurial zest

to return decades from then
as moniker: "nice shirt"

from that generation
of internet and cd

unimagined praxis
sessions of perfect sonics

engineered in a garage:
perfect pitchman at millennium.

"ON GREEN DOLPHIN STREET" [AFTER MILES AHEAD]

Even before R.B.S. 'borrowed' his mother Ann's Jazztrack album
I'd given this Miles "signature piece" to my own mother & father

She'd smile as I plucked the "repeat button" avoiding "his" baby grand piano
then I switched to "Stella By Starlight" in the slowest of tempos   so they
    could dance

the solos of Coltrane and Bill Evans exquisite glissando for they were young
    again
(even in person) over the edges of "entrainment" at zero embers of romance

then I found clutches of a bad listener   a tone-deaf woman who would not
    hear music
with no appreciation for "Intaglio" demonic   children grown up on   bad
    rhymes

'action and thought are nothing if apart' [these are the real births for which
    we die]
"love in a gesture   wisdom in a look"   warfare with no drafts over any
    flyway

geese sailing into the headwaters of reservations   toxic homelands
    (earthquake music)
(one woman I came to know in Iowa most literate district in the world of
    the prairie)

gave me "that look" with all melodies open every break clusters of
    chords   ovulation arpeggios   exacting   seizures the sweat at the
    wheel   an original squeeze

the matinees solo samurai war dance   even I could understand   with
   Mufuni
you could drink at the bar   swagger to a window out over the bay   each
   evening

and hear perfume art & song immediate   and already paid for   listen   but
   not touch
odes isles of forgetfulness in chorale "unfinished"   narcotic   "never to
   come again"

in any flesh you could touch or imagine in that cinema-noir perfecto-
   razorblade-bleed
memory at all levels of design papyrus repeat button to
   ensemble   Miles' etching

THE LIFE OF JACKIE MCLEAN

A critic 'trying to pass' writes me about crossover   played some   couldn't
   make it   got   his Ph. D
(he's onto new changes   an advance man   now active   in grants   from
   corporations)

would I come to Hartford and read to us the poems of heartwork all
   about Americana?
(I speak to Fret about duets—he'd like to come too—worried with nothing
   written down)

quibbling about money on expenses more fooled about crossover through
   the culture

(Fret still preoccupied with 'tenure' changes horns refusing to write
    anything down)

I remember being in town on a circuit downpayment for a house in play for
    another child coming
(I meet the doctor who breathed all night for one of my son's 'lost him' in
    SF)

$100/reading to make half a house downpayment with no gas
    allowance organized out of   Wesleyan
(but teaching every single class to the upper crust who 'vamp on spec' jobs
    already   pocketed)

conventions of "educators" in the audience   books to sign the world at
    bay illegible
(in comes Jackie but only to the atrium they call 'vestibule'   listening for
    cracks amidst   cadences)

I've already covered all bases of the tradition "Bird especially" born on
    grandma's nativity
(Fret is mad because he's light jewish bookish his folks about to split   into
    halves in the   stacks)

finally an actress asks about 'horse' when she herself stung ripe on Bach
    Brahms   Beethoven Buddhism
(Fret clamps up both axes as Pres cuts 'King of Swing' on borrowed
    time in Chicago in   '38 recorded)

King of Swing's rep never dies   Jackie leaves home   to teach build
    joises cultural projects   get clean 'stay up'
(the audience now kids in tutelage and bad   all races Dolly
    keeps accounts "In Walks   Bud")

BLUES FOR A COLORED SINGER: MILT JACKSON

Church music   never got over it
now called   'the blues'   vocalizer

found speed control early   as singer
vibrato like no one else   made you Dizzy

called back by Dizzy   in the 50's
known to be a player   of blinding speed

yet Bird's teachings   explicit practice at home
Dizzy's examples   make each note make sense

(two makes: one descriptive; one constructive
a tone of space   miscalled third stream)

Monk left room   Miles left mansions
John too mellow in vests   Percy at home   at hommes

my mother turned on   your version only
"God Rest Ye Merry Gentlemen"   at Christmas

her mass: full stop!   Django with few fingers
no hands   yet Bag's Groove   slight hangover

which stuck on your vines   liked you recorded abroad
symbiotic crossbreeding   instruments happenstraight

no chaser   Detroit called 'destroy'
Joe Louis diction   sitting in with all players

singing the blues   under your breath
right out loud   slowing down perfect pitch

in vestrymen   conversation
never heard such talk   in all registers   votive

banditry   in the octaves
overtones in   song   undertreads as thresholds

I loved you on piano   tranesaxophone
vibrobasshit   monkingus

chorus praxis   dizzynote
homemade choruses   nonsensical force made wholesome

INTERSTATE 80 FREEWAY RETURN

(Contra Costa College)

Ray Dondero Navy Commander recruited me in L.A.
"little sister of Orange County"
in 1964;
around the back surface road
you can see *munitions* ships
the children of Richmond
shipyards, over the hill
its twin, "Diablo Valley;"
one poem, "**Elvin's Blues**,"
called down Max Rafferty
on the margins of *obscenity*
and we are unloading
ships at sea
and at dry dock.

Talps, a cross between
monkey and pekinese dog,
provides the lessons
of South Carolina;
Ungaretti, the poet,
sorts her lesson-plans;

the keys to the grand
piano is in the failed
composer's hands in Music Bldg 'mews'
and *McCoy,* the real
Tyner, plays a recital
with Roland Kirk's
rhythm section:
the first Black History
class in the county.

"The roadrunner"[Travis Williams]
puts down his welding
for a few seasons(Arizona and Green Bay)
on track and gridiron
and without *Superbowl*
rings in ubiquitous hockshop   lobbies
for the *homeless,*
for **HIV,**
never reports to welding class
making his crease
in the evening cultural
programs
of 'disremembered' tempos "illegible."

―――――

LAST SONG [IN MEMORIAM: MICHAEL MICCICHE III]

―――――

Perhaps I pushed you over the edge
of the turnpike; perhaps not

my intentions(though honorable)were amiss
your search through 'intentional suffering'

your lessons in the contraries of the law
we grew up in(as a nation)are still negotiable

as 'legal tender' in the cash reserve of the ancients
while the moderns elude us   sage journal entries stillborn

your final examination in CHANT OF SAINTS was exquisitely
woven into extremes of 'gravitas' for McPherson's "Solo Song:for Doc"

alive in the actual tables of advantage you withheld
(hopeful as I was to write your citation for tenure one day soon)

now you are elsewhere   your own radio station on FM
my sacred annotations   of the possible   given up at lent

I felt your gladhand evenings in icestorms enroute to Massachusetts
Hall   on the floes to Canada in evil times

that zone inside you   outside your shadow [act] our map
in the songlines of the library reserve lists   a spring

Sterling provided to us all recitations aslant   in tears
(a voice like his distinct in any century up and back)

I would have directed you to the Woodberry Room on Harvard's campus
for you were a native speaker poetry of your song

as "Come Sunday" with no accompaniment in the bellows
what you stole in class from Jean Toomer   to educate the self

in days gone by leaders read the law(A. Lincoln surely)
to find the lingua franca of the state a modest tune

in any trimester stargazer is a lily   deep purple:
on that brief annotation of your life you speak still

LIBATION FOR ELVIN JONES [1927–2004]

He pours out the gin from the Yaddo window:
when in Tom Lopez's Fort Edward country studio

he mentions how the mic is almost random
in its placement   not like the bell

(Coltrane's he doesn't say)   on saxophone
and I know he's comfortable   can riff

as he needs to   "to stay up"   with tunes
in words the arc of every solo   phrasing

(I tell him under my breath about Elvin's
playing at Doris Duke's spread in Hollywood

how he sets up near the pool   refused to
dive in   his rhythms like even she hadn't

heard) but herd she did   like an ocean
liner on the prow   of her steady wake

'little catherine' who cannot finish her work
without placing herself at the center

of the chore   an emptiness no fingercup
can fill   even in country with small

commute   efficiency goes to hell without
some masculine attention   Elvin was "mask"

not to be contained by any session
(he could slay you with his zeal

if he wanted   youngest of 10 the baby
boy of the family   playing his mother's pots

at 2):
the ancestors are happy to have him!

DEXTER LEAPS IN

"there's not enough kindness in the world."

                    An ash, a maple
  flowering near Moody's
  'last train to Overbrook'
  on the plantations
  of the vertical: harmonic
  modulations of tone,
  hairpiece and scapula
  of church choirs,
  resonant, off-beat blues.

  You were sweet-humored,
  could kick in any register,
  but the horizontal measures,
  the melody,
  your tufted face
  as speech in Ella's favorite song,
  those were encumbrances
  if clutching was Jug
  and Bean in collusion;
  as for Trane, an ancestor
  in transition
  from the immaculate melody
  to vertical exposures.
                    Bud was there because he wanted to be
  (Glass Enclosures)—Pres wanted to talk
  about Hershel Evans

  but this was the Renaissance Club on Sunset Boulevard,
  a tandem of wife and kids,
  we were happy in the postcoital
  post office scheme

of big band admirers, just off 'graveyard,'
without a moment's notice to the police,
who were prancing in the alley
making our connections, the moneybags,
the jungle of chaos which was smack,
wilderness of trees
in the woodshed of prison:
sonics, for keeps, on *'Round Midnight*.

Happiness was not the booking agents;
the Watts local was gone, ogres
of the freeway are our battle stations,
so Wardell Gray was there to meet you,
and Stitt, conquering Bird's tunes
in duplication—you went far ahead
on the i.u.d. of the cabaret card:

to live and die on your instrument,
that was exploration
in the hemispheres, the hero's melodies,
the saga, acres of kindness in belief.

You could lose your voice, all things
shut down except the vectors:
"Straight, No Chaser,"
"Well, You Needn't"
planets in the yesterdays
of exile, penitentiary pleasure:
"All the Things You Are."

THE BOOK ON TRANE

In "Alabama" an off version of spiritual
J. Rosamond Johnson's hymnal holdovers

from his brother's gatherings in the field
James Weldon Johnson not allowed to beckon

his students into his Fisk 'sitting room'
because his wife has covered the furnishings

so JWJ stood at the fence in Nashville
talking to his children in creative writing class

ex-slaves accommodating only the highest plane of service
refusing segregation as a supremacist covenant

enacted to prohibit any development
except the group areas acts(in the fields)

yet he has built a church on these vestments
passageway etched in exquisite pain

only tone remembers   a scale untended
by the best technicians without the beloved's kiss

the vessel of song is the spiritual
the essence of singing the spirit itself "a love supreme"

A COLTRANE POEM: 9 23 98

On any highway in "Autumn Leaves,"
with Miles on mute Cannonball's date

you are in maple groves
in the high registers of song

ensembles spread in 'sheets of sounds'
critics parsed in paltry vocables

as you went on to galaxies of the unseen
"a love supreme,": *a love supreme*!

Human veils compress such longitudes
traverse meridians as tropical/sidereal

anthems in an internal kiss as a pieta
where the folds of this sacred veil

are seen as tributary to the unseen
and we rejoice in that *committal*

on a gravesite none has answered
as your instrument takes fluency   in leaves

clothes on the highway as flowchart bannister
the chorus broken   angel healed on bough

A COLTRANE POEM: 9 23 98 (2)

"Autumn Leaves" without a bandstand
  for your vigorous arc of light

  though it is bright and colorful
  in the extremities of music

  it is no ballad or blues
  affixed to the photo album

  and we are not in church in fear
  of resurrection in vinyl, cd, audiosphere

  and **Monk** is coming back to join **Miles**
  and **Bud's** *"Round 'Midnight"* is alchemical tribute

"Dear Lord" we have been slowed in our ascension
  figurations now energies of another *spiritual*

  this very day **Mandela** spoke in the atrium
  of a would-be-government-of-the-tonalities

  in tribal speech as in a Babel of taxonomies
  of our earthly kingdom now original

  and not in amber at the millennium
  but of the reed, and father of the reed

COLTRANE NOTES ON THE MILLENIUM 9 23 2000

"Alabama"
no protection still

that is not churchdriven
James Weldon Johnson's alternate tune

steep archival research
in playback of the melodies

wrested in church of the beloved
(no simple timeline in melodies

hummed at the vortex of a bomb
Birmingham   television hoses as carnival

reminiscent of Sharpeville)
what is African in us subliminal

as you discovered the soprano
which Miles saw that you had

when in France the makers of instruments
wanted to give him something   French

your kiss of the fluid accents
like no sorcerer ever heard in the vedas

mistaken in byplay as prayer
the intense registers of praise

high up in the registers
of salvation   all-knowing dross   in this world

if gnosis   is not forgiveness
already granted in the penultimate hour

(what does a black man on a foreign instrument
have to teach the world other than intentional suffering)

I would trust the pieta as parlance
in the free gift faithfully offered

as your compositions
transcribed yet unrecorded

in the vigor of a practice session
as the reed enables the passages of praise

all technical mastery
layed at the feet   of the high mode

————

SERMON ON O'MEALLY

————

this congregation knows about 'unreachable'
as it reaches for itself: *AMEN*

the archive of the present is **hip-hop**
most of it bad but timely   AMEN

spare parts of the voicings
'trained incapacity'   to riff with style   AMEN

as the masters did on solemn occasions
ritual death ritual rebirth   *at committal*   transformation AMEN

you have been in the fast lane of *Columbia*
bad housing plan with no parking(no leader of the **flock**)AMEN
        AMEN

keeping alive the habitat of *songbirds*
who no longer sing in key   warbling errant

still we try to echo the chambers of **arrhythmia**
by medication   therapy ubiquitous email   AMEN **AMEN**

without followup in protocol of regular mail(study the snail)AMEN
[**inattention** to the cost of 'service' rendered freely] **AMEN** AMEN

with no *Jewelnel* in the mix would have prevailed as dropout   AMEN
[her storybook ending to *Prof's* initiatives at *St. Elizabeth's*] AMEN

rare talk at Earl Hall in traffic without rehearsal with kid   AMEN
[**Bliss** in capetown apotheosis in spellcheck of coffin-etiquette *'optic white'*]

Hickman putting down his instrument for gerrymandering[his call] *AMEN*
[witchdoctor HAYDEN said: our *holyweight champeen* of your bad
    luck]AMEN   AMEN
again our twilight{**God's Trombone** and **Juneteenth**}to our
    ancestors   **AMEN** AMEN while we calm *relatives*   relations being bad
    'in late bad time'
    AMEN

LARRY DOBY

Saw his name on a poster
At Kenyon College honoring

Negro League Ballplayers
(remember seeing him play

in Newark in '46 I was a Jint fan
when the Bums brought Jackie

up from Montreal fought every day
at Ebbets Field   Jack threw me a ball

into the bleachers when they played
Stan the Man   Country Slaughter   Slats

Marion) Doby broke in when my aunt
Lived on E 97   what he took Jack took

But Doby had no outlet the writers drift
He buried all protest with his family

Yogi asked him to join the pta in
Jersey (kept asking him even before they ate

together as family) I remember the
Injun pitchers throwing at him until Satchel

showed up   then that stopped and
Easter was no St. Luke playing gospel music

Mays put his arm around Doby in '54
You could cover the alleys even straight back

Doby was a citizen when the klan
showed up in american flags smoke from their fires

On the trestles of jim crow funeral cars
(Doby carried his flag inside his chest Yogi said)

PANHANDLER (NEW HAVEN)

Out of Shell, out of Holiday
Inn, up York, down Chapel
this is a feast since Reagan

and I am without protocol
except to prey as I have prayed
on the angels on smoke, coke

the conjugations of degree
lost in Church Sunday School
which is open every day of this week

I came by cab, left in the wagon
my inmates at corrections
actors at Yale Repertory

setworkers for a meal and booze
on styrofoam hinges
on praxis and performance

no longer a student apprentice
and eating them as meal and token
I practice my lines for soup

and a smoke on acid-filtered
paper, stacks of silk
braided in get poor downturn

up in the sport vehicle world
I have prayed at what was once
a tabernacle, slept in a lobby

window, eaten with a fence
with connections to insurance
and the seminar world

In the stacks with a pass
you can stretch each metaphor
to a setting with no table

wares of the cooperative
world in the zone of fear
where hunger is never hygiene

out of gas, no longer inn
the underground garage
a lot imperfect, keys

in the trunk of maroon
plates, and a battery
to get out of town

out of nowhere
tempus fugit
bird lives!
[the loony tunes of elsewhere]

GALVESTON: 9 8 1900

No planes into the eye
slate and timber cut loose

bodies cut into
blacks at bayonets buried folks at sea

one   white   man   invited   a   black   family
to live with us   ever after if need be

surge took thousands
a wall of planks even Pip

could not describe
(silence the day after deafening)

Juneteenth not even a memory
yet ex-slaves stayed in the big house

Jack Johnson was already born
fixing to raise the standard forever

(thanks Jack   for that)
once was told to get up off a quaint chair

(before I broke it)
looks on the faces a watermark in a blink

for we are at sealevel on an island
that was never meant to be   blacks atethered

in another hundred years   an icecap
in a nightcap in a headrag the petition

no longer partition   but splintered
the bodycount endless on the dark side of storm

NOTES ON THE LONG POEM (*TUSCALOOSA, AL*)

'letters from an imaginary friend'—begin here
Edwin Honig did a class on this beginning with Lorca

the women and the men meet at scylla/charybdis
(your long suit is lyric grace   short shrift)

always begin with *metrics*   make them count
whether they can read or write   irmus next

lots of **Whitman** in Tuscaloosa many lessons
in guerilla warfare ala Nathan Bedford Forrest

all three volumes of Shelby Foote on battlefields
(Keats's letters   Proust   Milton   an exegesis

of Donald Justice's sonnet on Eden for Berryman's Iowan workshop)
Rukeyser Bishop Kumin Brooks   *"For My People"*

and **JUBILEE** together, Walker's dissertation on Vyree
(some Alice Walker student of Rukeyser tutelage)

make them study the industrial north Pittsburgh's
steel   the music of the hill   Homestead Grays   Josh

when it comes to the agrarians   make them translate
Bear Bryant always won at home new stadium museum

no traffic in the olympic swimming pool your lane
not many eating holes but lunch on the river dutch

best bbq is out of town   make sure you visit Oxford
good French restaurant in Birmingham   *16th St church*

documentary on George Wallace   **Owens&Louis**   birthmarks
Elvis in Tupulo angola   lunch on Natchez Trace

you will need AC in the endowed house already there(the parking lot)
get buildings&grounds for pine needles   now record rebel graves

who dug them
why the Big House and those shacks are so close together

JOHN KILLENS AT YADDO

Here in the summers; winters
could not breathe

summations of *Pushkin*
on the journeys in and out

of snow; the African in us,
in Russian denial

the court of Peter the Great
sanctimonious with speculations

about the prowess
of father and son

a worldwide penis envy
you enunciated with *Count* and *Duke*

on your vintage record player
each side man delicious

as homemade *chitlins*
(you would as what other kind)

but a Georgia boy becomes
a Georgia man

one evening, late
you mentioned Hayden's *"Starlings"*

out of nowhere,
wished you'd made amends

with him over politics at Fisk
'not recognizing his seniority'

in the parlance of the word:
"Amen!" I said . . .

HAIRCUT ON THE SOLSTICE

One should do this by the moon
the many phases: all grades of hair

Saturday in the park with batteries
if you have a salon gravey   choice stories

I'm in the barber chair with Rodney
his clippers zipping into the 'territory'

the wayward plots of hair in earlobes
(he's had to chase a bat at 1:30 a.m.

by himself with a net wounded he thinks
the bat's dead and he's through   his last)

He's counting the days to Tallahassee
(it was Atlanta   now it's North Carolina

there will be a move   too many books
his own among them   I've sent off one

to Helen Vendler   who wrote her book on
Seamus Heaney a few summers back) then Amanda

surfaces   went to private school in Cape
Town   comments on the shapes of heads

symmetry crowns   plateaus   then Mandela
the Belgians   British   all the takers

of stories   from the native   we're the natives
(Rodney says he's got a reading of Savannah

when Amanda says the South is just like Africa)
but he says nothing   he's already read   Toomer

if the issue is   CANE   it is about blood
we three chat in the john   den   then exit

TEN YEARS OF FREEDOM: SOUTH AFRICAN
FILM FESTIVAL, N.Y.C.

Major Visser had my briefcase in '77
Protea Station   Soweto   his manner like Stewart Granger

"Burl Ives" spoke in Afrikaans   for Basil Arendse's benefaction
Biko was already dead   "Jake" Jacobson(from Seattle)
put Sally Motlana's mail in the diplomatic pouch
(Ndawo had already slipped me the photographs of Soweto '76)
Percy Qoboza (Nieman fellow)   told me to pick from his box
(the passbook eaten in sweat and tribal location)

Table Mountain was where I ate District Six(Robben Island
was visible only at night   the gloss of pickaxe immaculate)
We were banned from talking "Mandela"
Winnie was down country Morris Isaacson was off-limits

"Protea" means cactus flower; I was to be beaten to death
without the 'honorary white' visa Evaton/Sharpeville
a stone's throw from Bishop John Albert Johnson's residence
"Fanny Coppin Hall" still the residence of women closed down

understand 'banning' was learned from the British
("they enslaved us," my papa said while writing his memoir)

apartheid class is as comfortable as race rituals at home
(nobody cares how you feel   the Constitution a slave document)
Thurgood telling the truth in dirty jokes for the Gourmets
segregated supper club and cordial "Shaw"alley heydey of talented 10th
and so I serialize Mandela's cabinet of inmates
keeping each other alive in everything tribal but "Afrikaans"

and when he walks out he is "strong in the broken places"
a King   a Prince   a 'terrorist'   whatever you'd like to call him

leading you and I from homeland to homeland: Sharpeville
Chief Luthuli's 'suicide'   HOUSE OF BONDAGE   Naude & Co.

rewriting the bible as oracular truth by circuit
every tribal zone of oppression somehow locus of resistance
so that "praise" is the mantra of Bantu
'musicians as artforms' libating the ancestors: and then to pray

CERTAINTIES

He goes to cartoons, then to the western;
in a suitcase, bound in leather, are pistols
used in a duel; upstairs there is a drawing
board, a table, the wine-cellar pop bottle
sits on the nation's prose, the summer prose
of the field.
            With a straw hat, and no brim,
he whispers about the east, meaning India,
meaning the sitar, meaning mountains
he himself cannot scale, though there is magic
in the hat, and in the speaker in the corner,
and in the music.
            The broken heart and the broken
tongue are the theme of the evening; betrayals,
in pictures, offered in court, the racist judge,
friends and colleagues, raised on literature,
unable to see the crown of thorns, the landscape,
a woman who'd been saved unafraid to testify.

Still the mother lies wounded, her heart-blockage
only the smallest problem of the savannah,
of the shells of the city, which are city walks
made by her fathers, of the buses that collect
tourists and veterans alike, at the hotel.

Hotels, viewing points of the harbor, the broken
city, marched over in ancient time, the hurricane
marching once more; across the bridge, viaducts,
railroad trestles, the camp where the first men
sat at attention, the sabres glinting in the sun.

Now you have friendship and good deeds, the moral
sector of the country ablaze in furled corn,
tassled wheat, the laundry of the world in a boxtop.

The character of such art, such wondrous speculation,
comes, at last to the jukebox; the laughter, adrift
in the cartoon characters, can almost fly. In Virginia,
the great names of the past flounce in the bible,
and near it, the graveyard, and the expression of soil.

And there are the trees, sectored into heaven
as a passageway down the main street, and the churches,
all white and painted, come alive in this song.

It is the song of the banjo, stiff as a board
but unbroken as a paperboy's string,
and it holds the news, the good news of a worksong,
the life, and the effort of the life.

    for James A. McPherson

HOODED COBRA EYES: BEGUILED BY PITCH
OF THE TRUE REED

"I don't mind the waterfall" BEING PREZ "but I can't stand the mustard!"

When Dexter said what he said overlooking the East River
I was listening to **TIME WAITS** by Earl "Bud" Powell

and thinking of **Monk** losing his *cabaret* card protecting him
the Hudson was *The President's* river in the apple

In 1958 I was back in town for the *Comus* and **"Six Pieces of Silver"**
and green as the sap of my Botany 500s on layaway

two suits and three pairs of pants my sister didn't cut with *pinking* shears
though hiding my car keys before my L.A. Times paper route was worse
    behavior

it took heart and patience to wait for that moment in short pants[kulots]
I asked her later when all grown up "give me an example of how I was in 50's"

and she offered *"you weren't talking to Dad"*   Mom was your relay
you would share the record player for my 45 then play your LP as even
    'Steven'

you thought taking me out with your *"just friends"* was a *picnic* from
    'punishment'
and whatever you thought about "Plato" or 'Bill' as you called them

"I shut up" only when I need protection why else marry two *marines*
and your records you *idly thot* so valuable you were **too** stupid to think

I couldn't count: catholic-school-girl in Brooklyn with perfect pitch
that picture of the **3** of us in Prospect Park in the 40's 'forgettable'

my favorite gift of yours were all three *Godfather* films on DVD I could tape
    tho   we have cable on our cul de sac of *Mexicans* selling oranges on the
    corner

Your students all sweet girls but not as sweet as me when I was *alone* with my
    father
I thought our *mother* had *iced* him when he left for LA in '51 Mays' rookie
    year

if you'd come back from *Iowa* for my wedding in November and "talked to
    me"
I wouldn't have married *Hillard* I wanted out of **2207** with my own clothes

the worst was my head in the toilet on Tuesdays and Thursdays at Dorsey
    High
after Mom dropped me off I would go in the side door of A Bldg & change
    spots

as you said to me once: *'between the dog and the tree'* is where I tied you up
Jon's *avocado* he wanted cut down his cat up Mrs. Q's tree and him cursing

[Prez liked to tell stories with his *plastic* reed: tenor or clarinet—couldn't be
    copied
the *Army* was the worst in Anniston barracks 'best' soloing with Basie at
    the *Savoy]*

what 'dead-lettered'your *airmail* at work-station in metered lst class:
    uninsured
your own *team* for four hours: canceling machine direct to the helicopter &
    LAX

The old man ran registry and could have moved up if he wanted to be a
    gaubee
but he was his own man at 2207 and didn't miss snow at 902 [Mom saw to
    that]

I love the sun and a breeze in the afternoon and going out for *porterhouse*
    with Joe Barrington who hired me because I could talk just like our
    mother in her intonation

No one knew I was black brown or beige and nobody called me snowflake
    even at recess

Now *stop* telling the world you braided my hair without hurt: "changed my
   diaper

so when I backed out the driveway in Dad's '58 Chevie (with Darwin in his
   seat)   puttering in drive to 2207, Hillard/Plato running down the street
   ass backwards:

arm reaching for my keys—he'd have died smashed between parked cars—
Mulholland Dr. took him in his Hillman-Minx: Aunt Ede's $1500 he had to
   have.

BOUILLABAISSE

My best student at Reed College
made this for a goodbye meal

mother-in-law thought
I'd run off with her (as her mother had 'run' from China):

then she was babysitting
my daughter but could not

breastfeed
nor calm her down

while I went before the *juryroll*
of the National Institute of Arts and Letters

with my *parents* in the gallery (when they were alive)
money I took as downpayment (*clams on half-shells*)

for a house I didn't choose
or want to refurbish

"then my grandmother died"
I was audited by I.R.S. and f.o.i.a.

the shimmy to the top of the *sandpile*
an unbraiding rope "of riddle and conundrum"

"out of nowhere"—Bird's tune 'on accentuals'
[Henry Street Settlement—my mother's unkept promise

where I belonged as a boy;
gangfighting recruitment of Nits and Jollystompers

as delicate as the *A.M.E.* choir downtown at St. Phillips
which held no place for me]

the story of certain fish
certain *crustacea*

where you could eat your fill
but not fill up

"ARS POETICA"

I would fly in on Mondays to Covington, Kentucky
make my way to the "Elliston" Room at UC Library

the students avoided the books I was stand-in
for Elizabeth Bishop   her pidgin on postcards delicious

her cups runneth over in Brazil   Cal's zone
E. Boston resistant honorand friend of Paz

yet Frost was first in line so Stowe waited
(made my way to Hillcrest Cemetery   locked

where the black people were buried
Ida Milsaps   Ralph Waldo Ellison's mama

then found her death certificate
"tuberculosis of the hip" misdiagnosed)

Cummins   poet and curator   loved to pun
his mimicry as bad as the food   black & white

from east and south of the Ohio River
where we ate sometimes on a raft   fm music

He was Huck   I was Jim   Twain was mascot
so we visited Harriet   her stolen antlers

I spoke of Lincoln   at the breaks   sent bad
students to Stevens   Emily   Ebo Landing

the stacks open and shut   like a Negro spiritual
nobody heard   nobody could sing

author of Invisible Man said it all as Braille discographies:
you must be your own spiritual father   (the vet)

BELLOW BERRYMAN JAMES ARLINGTON WRIGHT

What I can say about Henry Parker's tutelage and annunciations:

When dealing with Bellow his friends are most important:
MAGIC BARREL; sharing a house at Tivoli near Bard with Ralph Ellison

summer sessions with Berryman at Indiana: the periodic sentence
"To A Defeated Savior" as tribute to JAW's Ohio River suckhole

I tried this twice (and then again) in three poems for james wright
when I was commuting to Cincinnati as Ellison poet (Frost was first)

a poem about the indian burial mounds sacred to the indigenes
shared space with ritual grace with Robert Hayden's 'austere offices'

the 'critical mass' of my first visit to martins ferry ohio
the library on James Wright Place

he "ohioan" of his discourse with both sides of the confederacy
what is classical in hank parker's memory are 'old identities'

his respect for the local the neighborhood the modern the classical
as call as response to horatian miscellanies

part **THREE**

I DO BELIEVE IN PEOPLE

*I looked for my piece of bacon
when I awoke each morning*

*my father had already left for work:
the prime morsel of bacon*

*always there on his plate
waiting for me*

"Warren Harper," second of five children, and the most responsible, 1938.

POEM ON CONTENTS OF HARPER/JOHNSON KIN

for Kath

I had to tell you Leo did arrangements for Fletcher Henderson
(his club foot no impediment to his musical room   none could enter)

Our father tried to buy that house to keep it in the family
(his lookalike Patrice perennial student at Bard would visit Aunt Cora)

in Hudson where Ella Fitzgerald was entombed in reform school
Aunt Wini remembers traipsing with Ken and cousin Bob at Aunt Cora's

mother   Mrs. Williamson Ken would keep rambunctious spoiled cousin
Bob in tow (Ken could ride a horse and look good doing it

for some reason Wini not allowed to ride a portrait of Anita on her mother's
Irish cutaway a handmade table she would not part with   Hell's Kitchen be
    damned)

Percival died of septicemia in Chicago   a dentist   each filling killing him in
    pieces
(the grief of Minnie Serepta analogue to Nova Scotia waterways   and
    asthma)

I sat among the portraiture of our mother's reminiscences   Coney Island
M St. before Dunbar H.S. in foggy bottom   the color struck forever at
    bottom

Schomburg and the Bermuda triangle of preachments in a daybook only
    Rollie
remembers when visiting home up on the reservation of the Dalhousie

I trembled when I saw Wilson Harris from Guyana   saw my Uncle Barrett's
    profile
in an instant his first wife a blur in Bearden's collage   [Aida]   steady as
    Harper's

Ferry on the cushion of   Prairie View   Michon   born in Guthrie a
    puddin' rock
while traveling north when her parents had nothing   Griffiss Air Force Base

and Delta Lake where I nearly drowned by stepping in a hole   Barrett let me
    drive
(don't tell your mother or I'm cooked) three sunnysideup eggs

in Ella Mae's kitchen   her best friend   Eva Long (Josephus's mother) at
    pantry
in Rome New York   dead at Four Corners a deadly tree (River Rd) near
    Utica

HOROSCOPE: 3 12 98

"A work of art is a corner of creation
    seen through a temperament."
—Emile Zola

You are no girl scout cookie
                    invented in Savannah, GA
no FDR fireside chat either
                    delivered on radio in 1933
no Mohandas K. Gandhi
                    on a protest against British salt tax
no invasion of Bwy
                    or troops at Anschluss
no Truman Doctrine
                    no first ordained woman priest
yet you are a work of art
                    instigator of busy signals

in the mind
        where all play begins:
In this world
        you would swim off-shore
                on the Hudson River
right under
        Rip Van Winkle Bridge
            and pay no tolls
do no pantry
        at Dad's Dayline
           buff no counter
              at the Coffee Pot
                Hot Five
There would be reconciliation
        with your enemies
           but not forgetfulness
and I would still be your favorite
        nephew
          under the sign
            of Pisces
we will patch up
        all your injuries
          on the accidental shelf
and let you continue
        to shop
        for exquisite
          furs and jewelry
and spend no time in the cemetery
        in Catskill
          where memory begins
no railroad tracks to cross
        over 9 G or 9 W
          Uncle Ed's headbands

.

the perfect arch
         for radio
                 where Joe Louis
                         rights the world
                                 for us
"And I Punch Back"
             my daughter said
                     to my mother
but not in the cookbook she gave you: "kiss yourself," she said.

HOROSCOPE: 10 3 98

"don't work my fairbrown too hard"

Your mother, still light on her feet,
is answering while you beauty up the coif

packing some heirlooms only you can tell
and watching your back even at 75

56 adds up to 11 or a deuce in numerology
and you have been lucky in your cups and saucers

the best part of Omaha still fixed in your memory
and relays in Modesto where the Giants played

now back to the borders of the San Joaquin
as a waterway to vegetables in your own truck garden

if you would plant   and on the new job
plantation   for these are wages still unearned

in the polity of the marketplace
and you could be on the chopping block

if you were less smart   and still unwilling
to bend to the sacrifice   psalms and hymns

protecting you in the mercy of the word
'and I have heard you in the night without hope'

as you walked your way   into   and out of the sabbath
so commutation on the freeways of vistavision

are your solitary voice in choir   and in tune
and I will find the place where you live always

and see the welcome table and the welcome mat
on the upgrade   to the next valley   and home for you

DRIVING UP ON VAN AKEN BLVD

Buffalo black radio sometimes Toronto
Then a long dry spell Pittsburgh too far

271 you begin to look for Chagrin Blvd
my aunt's house over the trolleyline tracks

up to 3130 in to the zone of relaxation
from the road I stopped once from Iowa

with five white women in an Olds
(we all slept on the floor you fed us all)

from then on it was seasonal close enough
to bypass obligations refused any motel

when the Indians the Browns were in town
the local coverage was grand with pictures

around the corner was a doctor surgery
the rounds of golf penciled in the basement gin

I never took the trolley anywhere clang awake
All through the night you'd parcel out keepsakes

Your war correspondence Fort Huachuca stamps
"The wizard" on horseback or riding his mule

To Chehaw Station when you would not sit
Behind a screen in a jimcrow club car

Ate nothing while the crackers ate you alive
(you made me disappear as a boy in mama's)

kitchen I was screaming "here I am" at
the top of my lungs after naps I would awake

screaming early rage that had to be quenched
(the rest of my life I whisper at you)

MY MOTHER SAID: FOR MY SISTER, KATHERINE

"I can get over any death but my own,"
she said   to my father   who hadn't retired

when she had   left her in bed stand
when my brother died landed on his head

hit broadside by a woman in a Continental
who backed out into his lane on La Brea Avenue

he never saw her coming off on a tangent
for milk by a woman who wouldn't feed her own child

and left him to do it not his own child
(landed with his helmet on resuscitated

by emergency personnel never woke up
'dead on impact' my father took him off

the respirator after a fortnight)   wanted to
travel to Africa   with his brother   token at L.A.X.

the stop sign he ran enroute to the airport
traffic impeding his progress to go straight

My sister who will not speak of his death
even now   since 1977   said to me about our brother

wouldn't bend   never got the face he earned
not enough time   to look like our father

who was protected by our mother   not an old soul
and not about to be reasoned with about his son

either   then she started to sit up   crossword
the light on the pages of the times lucid

as they both did the puzzle   their retirement   *soft*
signs of the cancer that finally took her

had taken his father   who buried two sons
not knowing how either   first and last   left him

in his *memoir   I'M KATHERINE* which he wrote
to stay alive   even with alzheimer's hospice care

at home   would hum the **liebestod** as she had done over their boy
(and did so in her gown at dawn when she came at last   for him)

ROME, NEW YORK

for Josephus Long, in memoriam

My uncle pulled me out of a hole
in the creekbed at Delta Lake
when I thought I was drowning;
I hadn't swallowed much water,
but he looked concerned,
would explain nothing to my mother—
perhaps they were fighting
over my grandmother's house,
all she owned in the world
of progressive strokes,
those that marked my winters
of soap operas,
her **Braxton** body walked to and fro
across the upstairs bedroom,
where she could look out
on the one chestnut tree
that finally blew down
in a hurricane of '48 when she was dead.

This uncle got run off the road
and killed on a run from Rome
to Utica; all four of them dead,
a *strange* woman next to him,
the whole family trying to figure
just what happened
upcountry at River Road.

When I met his *widow* in the "Love Field" Dallas
Airport, with my son, Patrice,
named for Kennedy's *Ordeal*
in Africa, not to mention Ralph

Bunche, she could hardly keep up
as we changed planes for Savannah,
Georgia, just behind a hurricane, and so I sat her down,
took her picture, remembered
her cooking eggs, *"over easy,"*
in that same summer when I almost
drowned at Delta Lake.
    She was 6' tall, skin
the color of *tobacco* rolled up tight, her first
daughter, **Michon**, born in Guthrie, Oklahoma,
almost an all-black town
even today, where only Ralph Waldo
Ellison's *Invisible Man*
is required reading, and that because
of Roscoe Dunjee, the editor of the *Black
Dispatch*, the best keeper of record
in the whole country, for a time.

So Rome, New York is special to me;
it was an *'outpost of progress'*
in a saga of disappeared *chestnuts*
which fed a boy who learned to drive
on his uncle's knee
when the Thruway was still open country toward *Griffiss Air Force Base.*

MY AUNT ELLA MAE

She was the first to tell me of Juneteenth
her grandfather's holiday when she heard him preach

I see her singing in that tree of transformation
from "slavery to freedom" in Austin by the river

the library was segregated   never any Alamo
for us   she said we invented Texas chili instead

at Griffiss AFB in Rome New York   bacon & three
sunny-side-up eggs   my Uncle Barrett Johnson had given

me my first driving lesson   between his knees
we sped   I stepped in a hole at Delta Lake

he pulled me out   on River Rd   at Four Corners
between Rome and Utica   four people died

he was last   hitting a tree at a terrible
bend with no tombstone   I was teaching at Hamilton NY at the time

my friend Josephus Long   Hudson River School
painter from New Paltz   came to Esopus at 19

to work at Wiltwyck School for Boys   on the old
Roosevelt estate given to the State for wastrels

at retreat   I made them write letters home from 600 School on campus
in Joe and Lynn's salon in Back Bay   salmon my father would eat

on the dining room wall a cub scout and two
of the prettiest girls I'd ever seen in curls at Easter

I had a negative made of his print   gave it
to your mother(Michon & Cynthia) she had met my plane(not Love

Field)   I sat her down   "me and your uncle
had nothing when we left Guthrie, Oklahoma with Michon"

she then corrected the impression that she had "empty bed blues"
(she had the world she wanted in that old jalopy had met

your Dad at Prairie View   wanted me to know just how
we'd come to be together as adults   first cousins

my first visit to Dallas at SMU a white finishing school
she met my son Patrice   at   15   for the first time

she'd brought him a gift   more for herself   though she had
to stay seated while we sprinted off for Savannah's hurricane

her whole family   tall   dark   and handsome   smart
taught in the best black colleges   we did for ourselves

the ritual of "Juneteenth" always in my "craw"   this was
why   I went to a black librarian at U Houston asking about

that ritual   was told "there was nothing in writing" picnics though
went up five floors to 'archives' in the same building

a white researcher opened the file   my assistant(white)
gasped   Ralph Waldo Ellison called it 'trained incapacity'   (Veblen)

The Big "E" had written "Juneteenth" as the only excuse—in 25th QRL
for freedom   Reverend Bliss(almost white)   and Reverend

Hickman   (black   a jazz musician)   gave twin sermons
after Galveston   1865   the last place where Lincoln's

"Proclamation" was read to the ex-slaves   who would not be
idle   General Granger   who certainly could read

read from the document   some of his soldiers could read
many could not   your mother loved to tell me stories of the Brazos

(she was from Austin   I loved her accent   her poise
a sweetness   unknown in my native Brooklyn village   except

for my mother   who didn't believe in writing things down)
yet she wrote in a journal for you   Michon   and loved

your mother   as I did   her bacon grease   glossing
three eggs in her Texas skillet   Joe Long's mama   Eva Long

was her best friend in Rome NY   she took you and Cynthia
home to Texas when Barrett died   then I found you both in tintypes

ICE

"Grandpa cut ice at Catskill."

I think of him making his own
mandolin, prince of hell's kitchen,
the Bastine blood
alive in the cemetery,
the flu epidemic (Spanish Flu)
killing his kith and kin
like gangsters on the plank
before there was a bridge;
railroad lines
on either side of the Hudson
as trestles for the lost eye
that blew out of my head
in a pop bottle.

My son, born as the klan
picnics on my lawn
after a quick check
of the Birth of a Nation
will not clean toilets,
he will not shine shoes
at the point; he will not visit
his brother at Elmira:
9G and 9W
are my Tivoli.

You cut ice on the Hudson
to eat, and you eat ice;
some icefish, some iceskate
on the blades of the commissary.

I go by the house on Koeppel
Uncle Charlie bought for us;

I saw him first in Ithaca,
the only one in the family
who could pass for white.

Flo, my darling clementine,
are the guts of my mandolin:
I don't need to read to play;
I don't need to train to fight
the battle royales;
my training camp are the boats,
my brothers as seasonal gangsters,
and Mom the hardest puncher

SNAPSHOT

Finding a solitary shot
of the first born
you ask might you make a copy

and that copy is never made:
the original in your pocketbook

under the passenger side
near Sutro Park

(talk of the pocketbook
in the trunk goes unheeded)

and a view of the seals
surfers on suited patrol

the fogged in Golden Gate
are the tangerine paint

of a tangerine song:
when we return from stroll

the pocketbook is gone,
so little money there is no loss

but the copy is not made
and the image is gone

and this cannot be said
to the owner of the photo album
who happens to be my mother

And there are other secrets
between the two of you,
she gone before the mast

and you on it
deceptions of the untrue heart

are not enough for robbery
the casual theft of precious mettle

gone into smoke as the first born
remembers the tangerine song

in every clasp the book
its pocket candid camera

when all was young,
the rose without a thorn

in my grandmother's garden patch
where I came to shadow
finch, garnet, starling

and the rubbish crow
prancing on nectars she cannot eat

SACRAMENT

the book says 'old French' and you say "*oath*"
(deposits of the essence at the heart of this drama)

I did bad time in St. John's *rectory* with my brother **Jonathan Paul**
(the knees among the habits seldom do the trick)

I went to public school   took religious instruction   on Wednesdays
(he and my sister were enrolled in *catechism* at school when he struck a nun
    in the stomach)

rulers after that were for measurements of the **confessional**
(the sins I took began with the police at **8** who dropped me off the site)

I buried all anger my mother *episcopal* my father **catholic** in rosary beads in
    Mary's name
(then I married a woman whose **synod** was erected to exclude me and my
    kind)

mysteries of this procession are the facts   of flesh and blood
(I took the lessons into labs and trees at botanical gardens and the IRT)

And so you followed me into the underworld of *Freud* and **Jung** and anima
(I took you by the hand into the rhythms of your mother's *mysterioso*)

I knew there would be struggle much hurt *tenderheartedman* to come full
    circle
(and so he did   scream of all **encirclement**   mandala epistle/pestle   the
    seven rites   *to consecrate*)

ELIZAVILLE

my son moved off campus
to live among you   he's unlisted

in your post office   unknown   at 'store-up'
so when I find him   his roommate   all

utilities off   and unpaid   I throw my weight
around   peel off   a few hundred singles

push open closets   leaser   nyt outlet
(movie theatre   steps   where sprained ankle

worse than any break)   explained to you   klan
cell very close by   who would know where

you are if I hadn't made Volvo appearance
know you're hiding from more   than library

less than a furlong from your room   before
you wanted to commute by backroads   crow

to Tivoli   Sonny Rollins nr Germantown
where you could hunt up lessons on reeds

DD was orphaned   you almost so   avoidance
is not the thoroughfare   via Taconic   village

Dutch interlopers   train to Montreal   Hecht
Bellow Ralph on a special brand of hunt

quail is a game bird   Tuckatarby   pup
from Cheever   Vassar women   New Paltz fare

geography more than the bridge to New Jersey
Palisades a brand of battle   to republic

not a record label   or a screen   race records
you can't buy the charts for   without vision

SUBCODE

I'm talking about 'somethin' else'
which is the story of a woman

which is the name of a tune
the tune not the woman

the woman not the tune
(my son walks in to suggest the woman)

a shirt toned up suggestive of a tune
rune & rubric a strategic choreography

of your *Cuban* temperament
your attitude of inflection

on the makeup of your face
(one night you wore a dress

provocative in every angle:
I remember the tune of that night

wondering why we're not eating
at *chez Sophie* for breakfast)

I'm thinking about cds
I wish to record in my own voice

in *Tom Lopez's* country studio
making the archival charts

of *subcode*   when I was a young man
fearless of strata and substrata

born into an ignorance of the cost
of loving the wrong woman

making it right   the boy next to me
a man   grieving for his mother

while she is still alive
in his habitual gestures

crude and fastidious   his template
another *subcode*

those secrets by which we live
those secrets for which we die for

FIVE GALLON WATER BOTTLE (OSTER IS THE BEST): A STORY, A TALE

In the "best of days" there are three blue-tinged and heavy
(remember when my father your grandpa said "you should carry ice")

When empty they sit waiting for attention at 25 cents/gallon
(where and when "only you know" often stopped by 'vagrants' everywhere)

I take comfort in the 'hot' water spigot with "child" protection for 'no burn'
    orange
(the "carrying of ice" in the immigrant districts of Hell's Kitchen was what he
    meant)

The fashionable sites of Tribeca Mott 14th St. the Bowery stalls busstops
    B M T
(is what you remember on 'maneuvers' skipping school 'on the chase' for
    women: free)

'Don't sleep with women you can't take care of' was what your grandmother
    said
(the wisdom of downtown properties bought by an ex-slave were lost on you)

"Sacrifice" is what the ancestors knew and they withheld this folklore from us
(now you are caught in the 'therapy' of numbers: 902 816 "2207" 224/169
    1312)

The mythos of living "bi-coastal" caught on fm ipods 'soledad' "pay as you
    go" espn
(the shorthand of 'progress' deep in the bowels of the 'underground'—
    ferryman: song)

My mother saved 25 cents every week for a Christmas fund which she
    cashed in 1938 (to call "depression" a learning tree is ahistorical un-
    American contrite "purgatorio")

The math you know is epic chronological personal 'duty-free' yet someone
    knew
(protection 'pass' was literacy "progressive" statistics ice bottle quarterhorse
    quintet)

So I wait for you to 'carry the water' hot and cold to your siege-fortress-vale
(to live in a 'factory' for cheap jewelry was all the immigrants knew in
    Providence)

As tender-hearted and "soft" take you change the water: bottling for
    pittances
(yet by these acts one carried 'ice' into "Draft" Riots in the Civil War of
    freedom)

On both sides of the Confederacy: "it takes a helleva lot of nerve to sell
    water"—
(a woeful story 'joke' "double" counterspy double-agent secret-sharer:
    waterbearer:son)

[for Patrice, who thinks his father does not appreciate him, 'yet' feel his pain]

COUCH

for Philip Levine

I bought you in an absentee bid
in my favorite city (San Francisco) only American city fit to live

while I drove the smaller arteries of the valley   to Fresno
to give my first paid reading (went early to prepare to end badly)

I had gone to the Modesto Relays as a boy seen Willie White
beat Bobby Morrow at the Compton Relays

the valley boys 'out of the fields' were faster than the banked
indoor invitationals back east

and I had seen the Negro Leagues from the bleachers before Jack
Roosevelt Robinson baptized 'the Bums'

my father was a Giant fan and so was I reporting the ball scores
each morning

to my father's schedule after graveyard shift and now I would be
reading my paltry poems at evening

in Fresno. (I read badly and too fast and hung over)
but then returned to fogbelt of Miramar off Ocean boulevard

with a check for $75 and no expenses I could feature and the
couch cost $74   8' long on the 4' door roof

so when I sit down now in a new century on the lower level of a
converted jewelry Hedisan building

look out at the freeway traffic and off-ramps write the same bad
caesuras in a weak pulse

to the arteries of Providence Plantations think of the granary
the singlemalt I cannot afford recover this couch

which was redone by a man dying of cancer in twin cities carted
to another home I could not sustain or build any

better than an absentee bid across the continent of birth in the
afterglow of Roger Williams before slavery 400 natal years

while slavery supported all trade in the new world so when you
look up at chestnut beams up to the roof

think of new tubing for air conditioning in summer the pocked
brick arsenal against the wintry winds

remember this couch as weapon about to be couched in a field
of social security gone empty in war

to see the couch as battlefield cemetery garden truck and no
resting place but an extra bed in middle passage

WHY I DON'T DO SURVEYS

I have forwarded you a virus
and you have confirmed my disease

it will be used against me
(as it has been done before)

since 1970 I have known these corridors
(and ghosts that still inhabit them)

since my daughter was a student here
with keys to my office[1990–1994]

I have paid in connective tissue
the legacies of virus

I LOVE YOU it says
as I love them

surveys and surveyors all
keeping tabs on implements and supplies

while stapling every appendage
with a Brown iud# 010025768

calling as inventory
a silent pathway

to the arbor
where I have tried to sing

a true song
no computer could hear

and feel that song die
with every new challenge

of another survey
(if we only knew your needs we could help you)

when any nightingale, eagle, or crow
should know

when they approach with I LOVE YOU
it will turn into virus

infecting you and your song
so you will never sing a true serenade for anyone

"SLEEPING UNDER A WOOL BLANKET HERE"

for Dr. Ferdinand Jones up in downeast Maine: 7 17 07

At least you ain't alone: I wrote a poem *"Alone"* for Miles Davis in '61
(Trane died forty years ago today—I was in Mexico: Viet rice'n beans
    nuptials)

On a beach at Mazatland I ran into a surgeon on steroids from Iowa
    Medicine
(the blonde heads of his daughters glowed every night: *Eutha* his nurse-wife)

I buried all this darkness in *Debridement* in circular sestina at play much later
(In my heart was Trane's melodies: *Alabama, Dear Lord, Like Sonny, Naima)*

Even in Glass Enclosures I was without a book but bided Bud's **time waits**
(and death came a capella: Sharpeville, Kinshasha, My Lai, Cambodia, Biafra)

I made a reel to reel of *Peace Piece* to deaf ears: tonics of Bill Evans' solos
(what Kenny Burrell said about Lady needing Methadone in England to stay
    alive)

Heartwork is everything in the nation's music worldwide: 'Tivoli' Nagasaki
(I gave away my blankets in Iowa City when I left town on 20th Century
    Ltd)

A first-class air ticket from Cedar Rapids in a four day freeze uncashed
(the arms of *Weather Report* lost on Tri-Cities to gutbucket stand-downs
    shouts)

Into that oblivion of *"Good Morning Heartache"* I came awake finally
(the worry-music of my mother when I was in jail set me free)

PATRICE AMONG THE ELDERS

3 8 97

"If I could I would always work in silence and
obscurity, and let my efforts be known by their results."
—Emily Bronte

Herb Caen's luncheonette, the Moose:
we should eat here more often

you are composing tunes
you are afraid to write down

one doesn't know if notation
is signpainting or song

but it is difficult
if Ellington's consultations

McCoy, Coltrane
Bill Evans

has you in cloister
as a monk in his glottals

I heard you play the sirens
of Key West in springtime

the natives driven almost away
Steffi lobbing to you

and the nets were clean
as the no fault line

while you snorkeled
among the fish

piscean transcendent
off the showls

in *vitera bravis*:
return to the nest

where, like Henry Hudson,
you gave name to new waters

and like Joe Long, wise Josephus,
funneled the landscape

with indigenous pride
as in the Catskill graveyard

with your ancestors,
some of them from Hell's kitchen

their songs are good enough
you were brought forth to make them

trust in the spirit
which is your namesake

compose your song

GETTING MY HEAD SHAVED BY MY SON AT ODD HOURS

He puts out the bowl shaving cream from *Trader Joe's* replaceable razors
(he's drunk up my 10 and my Tanqueray with or without vermouth)

His mother could not dance but he can getting around the countertop full
(which he will clean off as he flies in and out from *Madison* on my dime)

It is not a dime I won't give though he tables my design for a schedule to fit
(the **tender-hearted** part of myself is clearly in his voice and
     attitude presidential)

Bard College and my many albums he took to memorize and wear
     thin razorblades
(because of his grace he takes on more than he can carry carries
     more waterbugdense)

I bought him a bat and glove for professional duty he had such a
     swing Mobile-ready
(then he fell under the spell of his siblings his **mother's** antics of woe genetic-
     dross)

He thought I was talking to him even when 9/11 hit he called my office
     twice
(c-span and booknotes dutyfree yet he was locked on NBC when the planes
     hit)

Nobody else could have made me *'come home'* the tone of his voice ecstatic-
     wound
(only twice did he cut my pate with speed and exuberance hurried lost on
     gin)

To kill the pain of *genesis* and the welcome-table of the genepool we both
     did worship
(the buzz is growing back I could do it myself over martinis **but not
     without him**)

GLASS (CRYSTAL)

Orestes by fate slays his mother
the mother beguiles the son

Portland the scene of miracles
the son just afternoon born brown

his mother's secret forgiven
(but by whom and for what   she knows)

her mother lies in another hospital
across town   she takes this son

without transfusion   after surgery
mother a yellow ghost   lays the son

on her mother's gullet   most of stones
removed   but yellow still   rallies

varises   symptom of deep hurt   lost
options   compounds a stellar heart

the boy thrives while his mother
trespasses   reckless is the path

she takes him on   his loyalty   brown
is with his father   who knows all

and nothing   for she loves another
withholding   all she is   true love

sacrifices   aborts   the shame undone
as hemisphere for the soul's meandering

the poet   father of brown boy
drinks from the goblet   light refracts

as prism to this storyline   frontiers
where the egg does not fathom the yoke

BERMUDA TRIANGLE: FOR *PATRICE CUCHULAIN HARPER*

{ & Bishop John Albert Johnson, A.M.E. [1857–1928], in memoriam }

The flight on JetBlue from Logan was through JFK portals not non-stop
(at high altitude and 'in the pink' sandy beaches Patrice pockmarked amoeba-
    rum)

The American Biography sketch of 1931 **JAJ** was courtesy of Ezra Pound
(whose *'mandarin'* was obsolete kicked out as undergrad for nothing
    Chinese)

On landing at the dark side of St. George's a windward angle of descent
(when **Hadley Woolridge** took charge in his Toyota taxi: 29 St. Michael's RD)

I did not sleep despite the breeze treefrogs desperadoes from New Orleans
(Patrice made me pump my fins in Celia's swimming hole *'unoceanic'*)

And so I thought of *Minnie Serepta Goosley* her doctor **Roland** dentist
    Percival
(the *"daybook"* kept solemnly from *End of Slavery*(Brazil) to 1892 a guidepost)

And so we found Bermuda College among the 'rosemary' oil & **St. Paul's
A.M.E.**
(Saturday's children streaming in for lessons on John Wesley's tabernacle
    choir)

Dredlocks of the poor bright in the sun all around the block the *'angel'*
    Hadley
(Celia Dawkins Manor & **USE TROUBLE** cd unplayable @ Paget @ St.
    David's)

The St. George's beaches coral conchsoup gingerbeer sacristy begging bowl
(duty-free in L.L. Bean dufflebag on rollers a parsonage-exit pulpiteer
    songbird trill)

The cost of a 3 day pass on a 21 day visa no trinity *Genesis* but tribal-triage
   ghostwalk
(the Johnson lungs asthmatic from all *Ojibwe* reservations in the colonies:
   U.K. stomp)

Time-share next time AIR CANADA from *Halifax* dual PASSPORT ready
(so Gosling's Black Seal Rum or Ginger Beer goes down BIG EASY trove
   duly)

PAPA'S DAY: NOTES ON PARTITION:
WWH: FATHER'S DAY GREETING '99

---

16 June Soweto: 1977
Wilberforce Institute in Evaton

a stone's throw from Sharpeville:
John Albert Johnson's reach from Brazil: 1888

through ANC formative docents,
the gospel of medical praxis

in gifts from all tribal elders
who spasm and infect the British

colonial visage: lovely world order
of Jan Smuts flowering in the gold fields

I say this to you in your 84th year
to factor in all you know you cannot say

not that you are withholding interest
on your psychic portfolio

just that you are greater than any speech
or gesture you could make

in the lyric space of a framed song:
and I hear that melody:

know that it will not end with me,
your line too long in progeny.

BROADSIDE

I have heard you sing in the shower   feeling at home   "at
    last" motherless   late into your thirties
(you went out early this Easter to get water for new growth   but not to
    sell as my chariot broke down)

When you were a boy we flew to Ireland from Oakland nonstop you were
    just two and weaned early
(Balleyvaughan was our pleasure with heated floors in the wintry
    wavelits near Galway Eire)

The chariot though broken without weight of a horse in storm of tether
    and saddle   was handmade
(My mother knitted a coverlet blanket sweater to warm your sinews   she
    knew as I did not an outsourced demon near)

JetBlue and Hilton have failed us   Tufts and Baylor have failed us advances
    in medicine   mother's milk failed
(in the snow we make our way into and through the arteries of
    creation(Venus/Mars) library exhibit in tornado)

Walk with me into the fields of hummingbirds in the lake
 country where   Wordsworth and Coleridge faltered
(I saw you leap onto the back of a horse named "Mary" unafraid your sweet
 nature fully known by a horse @ Stillwater)

When I was away in Jo'burg and then detained in Soweto the Afrikaners
 spoke bad Dutch about to declock me
(the prison of fear I grew up in was already a yoke of blindness from the
 good that you were as you saved "Ungie")

What could not be fixed was the zygote of her kid   hormones gone astray in
 the 'contrary' and called by that name
(in cellars in the haymaw in the bull neck thick fingers heavy toes Venus
 Apron soured of Mt.Lake   Sleepy-eye)

You will know my tone by the music of
 composition madrigal sonata aria the sea alive and 'ungovernable'
(I stood in Kinshasa at the post office in Dublin at Waterloo at Bonwire at
 Table Mountain in District Six)

The Keats of "Autumn" and the vales of soulmaking have not been lost on
 you   nor Eiffel and Pisa Message from the Nile
(this is the hardest vector of your life four decades that seem 'a waste
 land' incremental annotations of the dark)

But we know better   down into the very darkness   would destroy you is
 the hero finding his way home alone
(the light of instinct in timely distortion then corrections of dial in the
 riverbed rainwater and the firebird reborn)

(OMAHA) UTAH BEACH, FRANCE, 5 8 92

Sabena from Boston/Brussels has brought us here,
ring road of the "Virginia Hotel" close to the *African*
Museum, one part of the reason I gave **Patrice Cuchulain**
his name at the end of the sixties when all was promise

Paris on the left bank insecure, *Keats's* Roman desk mask
not fully affixed in Venetian mosquitoes in car park
as you wish to window-shop, buy gifts, transcend
morning sickness; we bought a car at *Schipol*: now rent

over the long holiday across the French border,
in resort traffic, with no bed and breakfast
open or shut and Antietam, Gettysburg, Bull Run
deadly in the graves across miles of ocean front

effrontery to *Graves, Bridges, Owen,* early *Auden, MacNiece*
crosses in the endless stream of broken vessels, broken wings
to battlecry; we drive south, almost to Portugal
but do not cross, even into Spain, like '68 into Granada

in supermarche comfort, at Armagnac, Reims, Chartres
we put off the *Sorbonne* until the end, sanctuary
of early tourist season a field of dignon, lost
engagement ring, found by chance, *chitterlings*

with Rhone red a delicacy incomprehensible in Richmond,
Portola, Oceanside, where I watched *OJ* traverse City College
turf, in penalty, a man among boys, until *Mays* rescued him
from Galileo High School, from *Hunter's Point,* Candlestick

You remember the pommard wine almost dumped out in first class;
we added the champagne from Reims, *lost soldiers,* King **Leopold's legions**

JOSH GIBSON'S BAT

Doubleday Field,
Cooperstown, NY

Empty at the corners,
the crowd bunched up
behind the backstop,
the screen, not high enough
for pop flies,
is crawling with kids,
not a ginger-colored coach
or resident,
on either foul line.

My kid, the first baseman,
with a pro mitt
and a hand-carved bat
made of ash
without his initials
measures for the fences—
He's got his 34"s
and is mad,
half the day spent
in front of coffin's corner,
replicas of the Negro Leagues,
and two hours in archives
looking at photos,
the thickest of Mays
and Jackie,
and they have his bat.

He remembers being called "Sambo,"
as his grandfather was
near Hamilton,

on the IBM Field in Oneonta;
he goes three for three
from the southpaw figures of speech
on the black and white scoreboard.

Like his ancestors
he's got a great sense of humor
but not the body of Mays,
too many tapes of Stevie Wonder,
the broad grin of Durocher
protecting him from the girls
who hide in the bleachers.

He figures to tool his bat
with the birthdates of these girls;
he says he cares about color,
the race music of his talk
in the tape measured records
of the Group Areas Act
unwritten in tar and feathers,
a stand of buttermilk
and a fly stirring the batter
for pancakes in the wrong country.

PORTRAIT OF SON AT RHINEBECK TRAIN STATION

(A Father's hopeful framing in his son's body)
PCH—Bard College (Rhinebeck Train Station)

Above the trestle a hawk
as the Sepasco Indians
might have seen it,
a pledge to the anima
of cedar, locust branches,
inlets, waterbrae
which could end at Valeur
(painters without brushes)

the Hudson landing nearby,
as generations of males
(at parade rest)

frolic on the Taghanic
Trace in the 17th century;

there are the season's books
on his car trunk;
he is struggling
with assignments
timedriven by themes
literary, continental

and wondering how to swim
on his own, frangible in light,
and wearing my lined
raincoat easily too big
for me at his age

I salute the bird,
a figure on the ground
in the trainstation

but east and west
of the faultline
before maps schedules:

in the best world his mating call:
her answer at the fireside.

PARIS

Most will see him as a spermbank for Helen of Troy Gilgamesh pinnacle
    revelations
(I will see him as fully-formed the last of a line refusing to beg for anyone a
    blessing   himself)

My parents found a wife for me in '64   in '68 world-wide protests nothing
    on film
(yet this boy was already making his mother sick in a brand new Volvo picked
    up at   Schipol)

How do you figure such music   license plate from Germany the clicking of
    heels at all   borders
(the aftermath of Great War with mustard gas careening to ideology Freud
    could not   fathom nor Marx)

The Continent calls for clarification: Patrice Lumumba dead! hero of the
    planet Leopold   King and deadly
(every turn across the hemispheres a new lingua franca to
    fuel minerals concubines   armies of night/day)

Still the hero rises above such classical tonnage such broken chords courts
    and   courtesans invisible
(the ethos of a true bill of particulars HUMAN RIGHTS on his
    flowchart rock profile   jazz persona
'Round Midnight)

He has been warned about all faultlines in the
    bloodflow Hegel Marx Engels Russians   American Phlox
Genghis Ashanti proverbs
(the ancient and moderns converge in transport commerce hegemonies race
    rituals race   relations
exotica-forbidden)

His own backyard is for the future both hemispheres a linguistic bank of
    Amazons cut   down enough fresh
space for no one
(migration internally becomes the sonorous music monarchies have fallen in
    French   revolutions world-
wide Presence Africaine)

The artistry and gnossis of the monks are not enough as scribes Kingship
    abounds in the   very naming
born at high noon
(sidereal timing in medias res siting self in the lyrics of Arts/
    Sciences Einstein   neuroscience of the brain
his sacred geometry)

MAMA: TO SON

Don't be listening to my records
when I'm gone

why did you kill your e.s.p?
because I didn't want to live in the world
at such high prices.

Now about those records

KATHERINE LOUISE JOHNSON HARPER

Visited Mother Bethel in Philadelphia on Reverend King's dead day
(inhaler in hand, the Johnson lungs seeking their vengeance, and windy)

missed my plane and retraced the commuter connection to Newark Delaware
traced a decade ago on weekly maneuvers: the path crooked but straightened

taken directly to restaurant to meet 'throng' including a late graduate
thought about John Albert Johnson's graduate study after Bermuda(1888–
      1892)

went to visit pews, artifacts, portrait gallery in oil and agfa brovira
thought of all his sermons at Schomburg; loved his daybook, thought about
      you

being pushed up Lafayette Blvd in Brooklyn an avenue of chestnut trees
first girl of many generations but grandpa fretful with your Braxton nose

light complexion 'blow' hair his refusal to be confused on same apartheid
      lanes
he had navigated in the missionary cause of Evaton (near Sharpeville)

the precious native jewels he threw overboard in fear of declaration:
Richard Allen/Absalom Jones, the yellow fever epidemic in PA with
      shortwave

shipping news via Sante Domingo: an entry in his daybook on abolition:
Brazil, 1888, what will happen to the monarchy(an elite colonial on loan

from Oak Bluffs, his Minnie Serepta a native Nova Scotian, where he was
      married:
all this told to me on your very knee amidst Lafayette roses:

they are archiving Mother Bethel's sacred documents, but not JAJ's Louisville
address in 1924 when grandpa proved no 'gangster' bishop   moved aside

despite his Freedmen's Bureau etiquette to Douglass's sacred effort(Lincoln)
first member of the elite AMERICAN NEGRO ACADEMY

honorand of Wilberforce (Ohio) :as you said when head to head with
    Sterling
on talented tenth of D. C. : all trying to pass for white

the blacks the only ones with education comfortable with their hue & cry
nursing their own and all the rest in an epidemic not of their making

"I can get over any death but my own" you said years ago
and when you did not recover from mega doses of chemo

let your mark on the cylinder of 'unknowable essence' esp   banana republic
in the jacaranda tree you brought out of Canaan onto Orange Drive
    ponderosa

today the ivory of the piano keys a delicate fugue to your bad luck
leaving your husband and children behind you   the grandchildren
    handcuffed

to the glow of your ritual concerns: I met the photographer on your 50th
    wedding: blossom too tired to fade with every pollen visible: GOD'S
    TROMBONE

Reverends Hickman and Bliss attired in the transition from Slavery to
    Freedom
as Juneteenth is splayed in the coffin of the resurrection:

uptown at Columbia University Earle Hall   lots of deferred maintenance
and your mother Alice and all her siblings(four)native New Yorkers

marveling at the gene pool of your transcendence: failing kindergarten,
smacked by a stranger on Gates Avenue as the trolley went gamboling by

the dark hand of the offender taking umbrage with your native Easter fare
swift and elegant hand none could copy 'the queen of love letters to warren'

and in the penultimate metaphor: trustworthy to a fault wine of piano wire
who loved Kansas City music   the Blue Devils on radio   air checks galore

'integer is a whole number' all the segregation you ever knew to forfeit
in the grand temper tantrum of race relations still buried in the public library

your parents promenading around the reservoir which became that library
playing your jacks on Sunday on grandpa's Germantown steps

shut up in unrealized democratic orders as you taught me to read ARABIAN
    NIGHTS
chance to be taken in ennobling enterprise to thrive on inner music

the art of it a cadence to the caliper Prospect Park   Savoy Ballroom
St. Phillips vestrymen too much animal husbandry to master in any
    classroom

one is always left back in the chemistry of essentials
moved forward in celestial radiance of one's own song

I was a hidden treasure and I loved to be known:
sometimes I feel like a motherless child

your mother sang it in rocking chair Weldon and Grace Nail
gave to her on her wedding day parading on Fifth Avenue as natives

when you make sense of fences   plots   in Cypress Hills
on visits to the ancestral graves   it can't be religious instruction

unless your Episcopalian, AME, Catholic, sephardic rabbi   Sufi
every part of the civilized world to be cultivated by your spices

at home in the wilderness of your creation   indigenes   from all continents
Maimonides record-keeper scribe stenographer shaman orisha

HEADSET

(in memory of my mother)

Rachmaninoff's Second is upon me;
I conjure all the opera music you knew,

how lush your contralto heart, how fine your gloss
of Kansas City piano music; how swift your frock

at the Comus; I watch you cutting papa's
hair; there ain't no hair like his under those deft fingers.

"Write nothing down," you said;
no notes fine enough, not even ashes.

"JUNETEENTH"

She sends these cds to me to get under
my skin   knowing in her moles   I'm dug in

likes it that way   thinks about her mother
knows her father would kill me   yet he knows

intrigue   in three languages   two continents
homestead   where postal worker was shot down

making deliveries   as swing man   nothing more
(when I go to the post   no stamp is clean)

yet the blood of this day   Galveston   Texas
for once written down   Emancipation   1865

Proclamation   A. Lincoln   in his own hand
(already dead when it was announced

you will not be idle   the soldiers said
many of them who could not read   though

Granger could) some parts of this world
it is a real holiday   meridians of women

collecting for the preaching   parkbenches
hurricane barriers   choirs   with no AC

I once put my head between your breasts
(the most sensitive parts of me   she said)

working my way down to the bloodless veins
up again to her mouth   scalp   tongueline

here is where you collect your weapons
in freedom   try to write your name   on her mind

INDISPENSABLE MEDITATION ON THE FAMILY TREE

I was born in the same house as my mother, and delivered by the same man.
how strange this configuration of the chestnut tree
how delicious the radiant nut; hurricane of 1948:
all the trees on Lafayette Avenue blown
then cut down; the Elks, who came to pay tribute
to my grandfather, his body laid out on cooling board,
paraded down the ample street,
and one patient-admirer-customer,
who called him 'my seal brown,'
was ushered into the waiting room

and told by my grandmother, Alice,
"you can have him now!"

This was 1940. I was "marked for papa"
he said on home delivery,
and Trigger, the pekinese,
ran back and forth under the birthing bed;
the mole on my right shoulder
marks the spot: love your blemishes.

My grandpa and great grandpa were born on the same
October day, papa on my mother's birthday
took to the cooling board; Alice said he sleepwalked
and was gentle being brought back to bed
perhaps remembering Bermuda
when his father preached and ministered
to the poor; when his ship finally came in
a roster of gentlemen from Exeter
were on the gangplank;
whatever happened to the "M" Street crowd
is pure guesswork,
and to be guessed at:
"seal-brown," and black with rage
at the Armory Show when he was questioned,
an accurate color tintype his exact coppertone,
he promenaded at the reservoir,
courting my grandmother,
before 5th Avenue had its public library,
and both of them trustees
having been married in St. Phillips Church
which bought apartments for the affluent
of color, in Harlem, before it was fashionable
to own property, a purchase of self
if and when you were freed from Canada
where you were born but could not live:
this was the reverse geography (fable)

of the above ground railroad
taking your relatives to Minnesota
from one reservation to another
Ojibwa to Chippewa
what's the difference;
in the homelands,
at the watershed
at the source
boundary waters
of the Mississippi
you cast your lot
with 'the people'
in spiritual terms
and waited, defending
what you were,
or took to the word
of your fathers
and put meat to metaphor
delivered your own children,
breach or no breach,
you turned your offspring
around in the womb
to bring them back alive.

THE LATIN AMERICAN POEM

'geography is fate'
'how I came to know it'
'do nothin' tell you hear from me'

I wish I could be a citizen said the slave
in 1888 at the end of the monarchy

does British Guiana qualify quartermaster
faith in Dalhousie Ojibwe antecedents

"Well You Needn't" theonliest Monkey
'round midnight sphere middle name mojo

Odd /Fellow 33rd degree UPAS TREE Wilberforce
witchdoctor Amistad conjo Bahia Bahia Bahia

condemble St Elizabeth's anacostia natal proems
crazy rhythm asiento German Southwest Africa

Orange Free State Transvaal Besutoland
Bechuanaland Natal Zululand

Douglass Hospital American Negro Academy
masonic order masonic orders odd fellows

condemblé oh mary don't you weep don't you moan
Angola Angola Angola Elmina Elmina Elmina

border I love to cross in the deep forest
ghana griot sets rhythm at five master rhythms

afro-pop recording only the surface of modes
commanding Aesop to fable stable of folks

you like Lima, black, you like Rio, black
you like Quito, black, you like Neruda, black

Paz, black, maps, black, Cuba, black
you like Caribs, black, you like Cape, black

golden stool, not to sit on, Palmares
not to love on, maroon freelance samba

runaway songs songs songs alamode
bush bush bush griot griot griot

new world old world triangular world
kente kente kente rum rum rum

Dutch East India Company homeland bouille
base cockrey conch cannibal global warming

tropical equatorial fo'cicle griot
archipelago labyrinth Akan

white white white black black black
jaguar jaguar jaguar man man man bush bush oasis: Egyptian

AIRPORT

Are you late to pick me up or just late
to the car rental

I had given up on you finally when the
pace of auto traffic

within the lines of electric fencing turned
sour then light

bob of her hair idle plants of unpatented
feet arched sinews

excitement back in lumbago arch the
pockets of anticipation dead

but only for **moment's notice** (tune
memorized for lovesong

this girl knows by heart in Spanish
unless you eat cheap)

I gave away my key to **heartwork**
(thought against it/took it back)

ALTURA

The scar in your forehead
("the worst night of my life,"
your father says)
and we move on to the road,
by the neighbor horseman
policing the vista,
the light snow cover
from above, national
forestry in trust,
like a fired canopy
burning from above,
or so the experts
report at the fire station.

And it is high, a thousand
feet above the high plain
of Missoula
to which you return at Xmas;
so good are you at skiing
downhill, that you sometimes
forget the headlong plunge
down the mountain road
which endstops at the gateway
to the forest,
a wilderness of concern,
and the one horse
you shared with two sisters,
one in a veil,
the other at contract
with a newborn on her lap
in the apple
which is nobody's homeland.

Remember the state guide
with flora and fauna
you could recognize
in black and white
contrast to the slang,
glossary of pioneers
who could never be Indians

and we have your scar
in your forehead
as marker to self-esteem
which is regard for the body

when the mind has gone off
to nurture the soul: *bear, wolf, owl*

We call this poetry
and so, when you let Dunbar,
by no permission he could earn,
into your bunkbed
in the dormitory,
you did so for the soul
of his baby he should have carried
when he asked
without love
for your body.

So you homestead in the east
near your sister
and wait out the displaced
bungalows, downwind,
from Altura,
which is the endgame
of parental concern.
Blackfeet anima shamans.

You can see the world
spirits made,

the treelines,
south of the lightning line,
dry lightning
of summer fires,
the hose on the roof
to wet down the shale.

And there is offspring,
worthy of your gesturing,
on e-mail to home,
and your loyalty
to black frat step-dancing
in the segregated quad
at school;
you are nobody's
girlfriend, a future wife,
the complement of the rise
in a deadend vista
going home;
it has a turnaround
and sober, with light
and chronic Xmas song,
there is reenactment
in the pike position,
2 1/2 somersaults,
in the up position
with a pure landing
in a snowbank,
in pineneedles,
in the quilted protection
of your newmade vault:
awake now, to the elements,
motherlode of the self,
(your mother's aroma)
Altura, the high plain
where deadends are leaps
of the synapse: forehead, skin

MAROONS

When you left the ***Brown Providence Plantation***
I tried to pull you back to *Bristol*   Newport   mansions

Poetry teaches belief in people
it chooses you   you don't choose it

I saw you reach across continents of **TransAtlanticSlaveTrade**
I saw your brother *die*   your sister *broken*

I saw you heal in the ***broken places***
fly off to Brazil   Paris   Miami   Madrid   *London*   *London*   *London*

patterns   of *caretaking*   miraculous
the sure bullet in the *magazine*

I did not see you take such aim
for the care of ***self***   (I tell you now)

the isthmus across our languages   mestizo
Bahia Akan   Cuzcos *"Asiento"* ***Gullah***

our ***Ebo*** landing toward   *"intentional suffering"*
(I reach for you across these tropics

for once I close your mouth with ***Zulu praise poem***
for once you are ***my*** subject matter ***for the ancestors***)

this metaphor will do   **heartwork**   **to heal**
heartache   the chambered work   ***for us***   ***for us***

centuries ago   ***maroons***   set up camp
I see you travel from fire to fire

290

WHEN I WAS A BOY

I

The old man came home woozy
on only two occasions,
once on gin,
the other when his wisdom
teeth were pulled;
his great blueblack coat
had wide lapels,
a one button roll
in the snow on the stoop,
dizzy from shoveling:

1947 blizzard,
the chestnut tree
gone down in the high winds,
the Giants losing to the Dodgers
in Ebbets Field.

II

I would report the *'play by play'*
to the old man
during the desegregated war;
he will report to me,
if he speaks from the sore
neck I clasped about him,
the ice box,
of which he will not eat tonight,
mad over confrontations
of trash and chores,
the hype of the superdrome,

as if a man knows
he's a "boy" all his life.

III

"Madison Square Garden" chews he breaks on set teeth:
woozy on each occasion, beefs with strangers
or keelhauled: the Nits, Jollystompers, P.A.L., St. John's nights,
to confession, religious instruction 'Wednesday' afternoons,
subwayrides to Henry St. Settlement for free lessons never begotten,
"Snowball" and the Janangys, Frank Kelly, the Wibecans:
steady and brief encounters at Tompkins Park,
(where green handwoven sweater was taken right off my back)

IV

the old man tanning me for tossing a 'snowball'
right through the stalled window of a local fuel truck,
caught in the vice of the driver,
who delivered me to homestead stoop, vestibule,
handholds of the old man's praxis
to the third floor perch of downed chestnut trees,
(no longer visible, widest street in all of Brooklyn,
no longer 'home of the elks parade')
three stolen camels or unfiltered 'Lucky Strikes' at the windowsill,
the spreading of his belt
over both arms of 'the rocking chair,'(Pop's rendition)
a family heirloom my little brother always sat in:

V

stunned by the old man's tactics, my brother's silence—
not about to confess or be 'broken' by any plea—now that grandma was dead—
who seldom spoke up in strokes of quiet anyway—his feinted "backhand"—

mama at "Maimonides" Hospital, no ounce of protection but with her paycheck,
delivered to the old man(always good with figures):

VI

to swollen teeth and gums.

PULL-UPS AT PS 25

---

for Elroy Clark

Where are you, *king*
of chins, who, on any
given day, could pull
your *gibbon* trunk,
your spindly legs
50 consecutive times
on the mastings of the **flag**
someone else raised,
mornings and evenings
in military calm?

"Orang," the bicuspid blonde
with looping earrings
expelled, under her breath,
and without the long *reddish*
hair, you could have leaped
into the *arbor* of trees
if the fire escape landing
had not broken your *rhythm.*

As the toughest thug
on the block,
and in charge of the **flag
squad**, you once
walked the four floors,
equivalent to the gymnasium,
in **handstand** position;
it was rumored,
without any evidence needed,
that you had *fathered children*,
only an eighth-grader,
of *indeterminate* age,
but with lats and *deltoids
like Sampson,*
if *Delilah* was near,
and bicuspid was nearer
and you were our *myth*
of an antsy class,
heavy in transition,
before **gangfighting**
took over; and I was
on my own, after school,
free on a pass from flagsquad
because you had arranged
your pull-ups, and my flight
off the campuses of the world
into the underground BMT, IRT
and a pass to the Staten Island Ferry
on every jewish holiday,
which we both took off,
for I was your deputy in crime and truancy,
doing your homework and math for nothing.

And this *flag* I raise to you,
escape-artist, 50 colonies, (***E.Pluribus Unum***)
for saving my ass from the trees.

[Public School 25 at Lafayette and Summer, in Brooklyn, New York, was across the street from my great aunt, Edith Braxton Ford, retired schoolteacher from Hunter College, a native New Yorker, and oldest of five children, two girls and three boys, my grandmother Alice the youngest, had the first assignment as a grammar school teacher in the Brownsville section of Brooklyn, seat of "Murder Incorporated," and the Dutch Schulz mob, men of whom she taught how to read, compute, and comport themselves properly with manners. She taught for more than four decades, and was fearless. She was 5' 1" and known to flash her cane to stop a bus while crossing the her street, and lived at one of two brownstones her father, *James Randolph Braxton, a slave from Orange Courthouse, Virginia,* had purchased for cash, 902 Lafayette Av, where me and my mother were born, delivered by my mother's father, a Canadian doctor, Roland Rufus Johnson, M.D., and 816 Lafayette Avenue, residence of my Aunt Ede and her husband, John William Ford, a dentist, born in Orange Courthouse, VA, whose practice was in Newark, N.J.

His best friend was Jack Nail, brother of Grace Nail, and brother-in-law of James Weldon Johnson, who died in 1938, the year I was born, in a traffic accident in Maine, while he was on vacation from Fisk University, Nashville, Tn., where he was 'poet in residence." The Johnsons gave my grandmother, Alice Braxton Johnson, a rocking chair for a wedding present, which is still in the family. My father, *W. Warren Harper*, caught much of the tone of Brooklyn during the depression and after World War 2, in his memoir, *I'm Katherine*, 1993, privately published.]

HIVES

(San Francisco) for Nicola Boynoff

Eyeglasses
ala coke bottles

his doctoral thesis
still undone

we entered the cave
of Contra Costa College

his domain
really U. C. Berkeley

but doing time
on-the-job-training

on the children
of the Richmond Shipyards

There was Travis Williams
roadrunner of Green Bay Packer fame

Pamela of the hair
all of them drifting on Plato

So I broke out
welts and worse

instead of throwing him
'corrected dangling modification'

on his commentary
of my penmanship, logistics

what policy he makes now
in the regency

how fine he sees
munitions in housing

son of Max Rafferty
sheriff of Pinole

who can say
student of 209

November, the election done,
"the Green Hills of Africa"

no longer the grapevine
nor vineyards at Napa

IOWA

Lawson had his liner notes
and two copies of Kind of Blue

afraid to turn it over
so bad was side one

we used music in Iowa
to fight back grey days

with no horizon
you could not tell time

still we played
side one

over and over
and one day

Lawson came next door
a look on his face

saying "what's that?"
I showed him the album

held it up in silence
"kiss my ass,"

he said,
"a two-sided record."

This kind of fear
is classic:

he went back to his hole
I went back to mine

marveling
at a deuce in change

MY MOTHER'S BIBLE I

Michael Steven Harper
born March 18, 1938
at 1:25 P.M. Friday

Jonathan Paul Harper
born May 17, 1941
at 9:38 A.M. Saturday

Katherine Winifred Harper
born June 6, 1943
at 7:08 A.M. Sunday

Your father, **Roland Rufus Johnson's,**
Christmas gift
(you have his handwriting,
    the first girl in generations;
    when you call him *papa*
    he smiles; he can be
    "black with rage,"
    a feat for a copperskinned
    Canadian physician
    who delivered us
    in his own home)

Your sister, *Alice*
Elizabeth, has a similar bible,
both inscribed
your cover scuttled
(replaced by black
    calfskin, Indian paper;
    the **caduceus** your marker
    on purple ribbon
    only an *AME* Bishop
    from Mother Bethel
    in Philadelphia,

your grandfather:
John Albert Johnson
from Oakville, Ontario,
missionary
who bought the only
freehold land
in South Africa
1908
before the **Union**
became the union)

Your brother, *Barrett*
Rufus had Bishop Johnson's
bible as first and only son
(married Aida
     married Ella Mae
     his death at Four Corners
     on River Road
     south of Griffiss Air Force Base
     unrecorded)

"write nothing down"
you said
as the framed tale
to my *Arabian Nights*
which you taught me to read
before I went to school.

You sometimes spume
through the waters off Long Beach
as a Neptune Society
with my brother in tow
before the ashes hauled
and the waters given;

I thought I lost you
in the breakers
at Coney Island,
witchdoctor

numerologist,
"tigre" with nine lives

you were *episcopalian,*
my father *catholic,*
the three stooges
baptist (Friday/Saturday/Sunday)
because of the *singing;*

you are listening
in a storefront
delicatessen
on Lewis Avenue;

you are the jacaranda (watering your plants)
on Orange Drive;

a torn cover
          stitch by stitch
in the blankets

                              of your 12 *grandchildren;*

tropical
      or *sidereal*
astrology
      is Fats Waller's
choruses,
      lieberstod
the heartwork of nappy edges
          Ruth, Ezekiel
the **23rd psalm:**

an old soul
      in an old testament
is *mercy*
      in the new age:
why so many *eunuchs*
          in these
                    Arabian Nights

MY MOTHER'S BIBLE II

No one wrote like her,
each one of her children

on its own page,
births, deaths,

marriages
held together

by a royal ribbon
and an anchor

from her grandfather
the bishop

who forbade her from playing
jacks on the sabbath;

made her come indoors,
though proud to walk her

up Layfayette Avenue
under the chestnut trees,

her bonnet
framing the Braxton nose

and the Johnson lungs.
In the year of the tiger,

1938
in the Chinese calendar

I was born
33 hours in labor

delivered by her father
with two dogs running

under the bed:
"look, he's marked for papa"
Dr. Johnson said

about the mole on my right
shoulder;

and I watch the mole
in my 60th year

for enlargement,
discoloration,

a keloid, a recessive hair
as one is fricasseed

in the holding tank
of the family pantry

where one does laundry
or scutlery work

or tells the story
of missionary work

in the veld
before the union

was the union.
I took this book

to the Transvaal
and out of Africa

to Latvia,
onto the Natchez Trace,

into Tuscaloosa
'on green dolphin' street

our favorite psalm.

PIGEONS

In this neighborhood the man next door
spreads breadcrusts in his driveway (riddled with cars)

Mexicans and blacks are not compatible
but the birds flock into my yard for dogfood

today "Cleo" is adrift in the havoc
(will not eat those she kills)

master of this house almost lost an eye(new glass lens)
did two tours in 'nam(rehab a continuous dna mantra scrub)

indelible cleaning of bodies in bodybags in detention
(defiant 'eating of sandwich' in macho disregard)

losing his front teeth(blindsided)to be dragged off
his CO with a stool used as battering ram

on maneuvers(patrol) in safeways target von's fedco
(no children safe behind him in his wake loud noises deadly)

riding shotgun in home neighborhood in 'security' togs
pigeons on the revolving spit   inedible

CARETAKING SUPREME

for my sister

We lost our brother Jonathan in 1977
(I was in South Africa and did not hear)

Our mother began to fade from then on
(Liz answered the call from an unknown

assailant 'who dialed' to apologize
for backing into his pathway: Continental)

Even with a helmet on you can't sustain
headfirst flight onto pavement

Our father took him off 'life support'
(he also began to fade but took his luck

with sleeping with our mother as grace
the kind we said over meals mechanically)

In 1988 our mother left the premises
(I heard the call in the night moved

little until Kaiser called to remove her)
You and I know she left her body

long beforehand her whispers were shots
of adrenalin to your steady frame

I saw you rush to her protection without
comment the kill in your eyes and cadence

under your breath your instincts were deadly
(from then on you were married to two men)

Symmetry on this conundrum no mercy
anywhere as in a lost detail commissary

no recompense from purgatory no contrition
large enough to hide your very own Vietnam

As you approach your 62nd year
we must discuss the next phase of your life

'born with a veil over your face'
said the fortune-teller on Olvera Street

"in my father's house there are many mansions"
your knowledge of scripture exacting

psalms you learned to recite at catechism
the guile you learned the hard way at school

I thought you would keep your own house
with an endless bay of warm water cruises

you learned to love when you were off your feet
(with service everybody in white or nearly

so the tone of service 'out of africa'
the order of the godfather firmly in place)

Firm knowledge of film as comfort zone
to the long perfect ending consequence

faultline revenge a subtle tension
from the old testament Mandela prince

of prison King sacrificing all to avoid
a bloodbath when those who cannot be forgiven

are letoff free truth and reconciliation
(I would make you "judge" of such proceedings

and watch you work kinder than you know
so much like our mother subtle from left

to right side I am reminded of our grandmother
who died in '47 with no convalescence ever

the secrets of our parents where they lived
what they hoped for for us I see it now

in your lovely touch and blended presence:
"strong in the broken places"

our father for whom you care in trust
is off his game medication not quite himself

"I can get over any death but my own," our mother
chortled for she was saying goodbye as you will not

no quit in you "control freak" I badly called
when you were never carefree or careless

in your close minuscule monitoring cellphone
'round your neck raft from whence we won't let you sink

THE PATRIARCH, W. WARREN HARPER, CIRCA 1938

Part I ("there was no scholarship at Syracuse for a black Catskill swingman")

with the **Civilian Conservation Corps**
segregated *"camps"* behind him"

Williamsburg, Virginia [**"don't drive that truck within the city limits"**]
and his black brethren 'to work' the sand dunes beside him

this photo of a man in a plaid shirt forgetting the *"Coffee Pot Hot Five"*
while all played in a ***net*** enterprise backed by gambler Uncle Bill

who lost all his loot on bets   on bicycle races
the men on the take in Greene County ate free meals at *'The Point'*

without the old man knowing—*for I kept the register*—everybody paid
then **3** two-minute rounds with "Charlie" in *family battle royal*

in the wet basement
no towels dry enough to pick the oldest son off the floor

with just enough tips held out from Jack *"Legs"* Diamond's cigars
his parents went off to *Elmira* to visit their first born in lock-up: heisting cars

the shame of it buried amidst the chickens of *Ithaca's underground railroad*
for they were "on vacation" from the homestead runoff at Catskill Creek

Part II *("in dreams begin responsibilities"—Yeats)*

I looked for my piece of bacon
when I awoke each morning

my father had already left for work:
the prime morsel of bacon

always there on his plate
waiting for me

CATHAIR ON HIS BLACKWATCH JACKET

Fastidious
with agility
of her tongue
he gets blonde
hair on his jacket
his woman bought for him
in their best time;
he wears it in comfort
to sport her warmth,
an endless strand
of her hair that is not blonde.

But the cat's blonde,
doesn't belong to him, or anyone,
as she does: bright, crystal pendant
with masking tape for her tail.

MANHATTAN BEACH

Two hours before the setting sun in the west
(one has to be reminded which coast is coast
when you have set your father's ashes into the sea
where your brother and mother have gone before)
you are in the arc of the beloved angel on earth
and she has your jacket around her around you
you think of Rumi's sacred geometry in Konya
you feel the sketch of the sufi at cards
who restores the cloak of the archangel
his power drifts over you both skimming
the darkness as a shroud finally withdrawn
in her deft arms you might sing true
with the fire restored you waffle no longer
about the meaning of her flesh what stands
behind her such faith spirit music glow
the void only she can fill remind yourself
in the low zones of repression she is light
shared lovingly this has always been so
'you are in the service of the beloved,
why are you hiding?' this is her answer...

HOMAGE TO FLIGHT #103, PAN-AMERICAN

I watch my own son walk off the rib
and skin of the plane on the day of the threat,
and not go down in smithereens
over Scotland,
malt whiskey, rolled oats,
on the battlefields of the covenant,
where armies strode in their code of arms.

We will clean up debris
sifting for evidence
(a few money orders, travelers cheques,
changed hands in the forest and fields)

and these children who found the tender
children who placed the bombs
in the kits of the cockpit
or lavatory:

it is a cabin fever we will live in forever,
darkness, patches of phosphorescent light, darkness
in the common field of battle station
cemeteries aglitter.

COMMENCEMENT ADDRESS:
FOR JONATHAN PAUL HARPER (1941–1977)

Rhode Island College: May 17, 2001

My brother would be 60 tonight
we should be feasting our ancestors

none of them in Providence Plantations
he would have given up his yamaha

(plastic surgery would do the rest)
rest would be an audience at commencement (not Roger Williams)

his big brother reading poems on his natal day (not URI)
(needling him into childhood antics)

locking himself in the basement bathroom in Brooklyn
a cigarillo from our parents bedroom aloft inhaling

an occasional chestnut from the very trees of '48 hurricane
outside the window grandma's backyard roses michaeltree tintypes

you did cut Rebel's collietail with pinking shears
you did collect garbage follow fire trucks steal their uniforms

at the fire station you did steal milk from neighbors
(the cream waffling topside alongst your parched lips

you did race Muriel Burwell in a short dash to PS 25 playground
later to push her off her bike outside St. John's mass

(she was a Baptist   a choir singer   her hair
pressed into moist fingerrolls you had to touch)

astride your baton on the curve she ran you down
effortlessly a scissor in her hand

to stop you cold the devil incarnate
her baptism finished under water the homecookin' of your lunch

our mother never saw you born in a hospital knocked out
while I was born at home delivered by her father 33 hours labor

Trigger (the pekinese) under the bed in perpetual watch
while you were attached to our sister born in 1943

Katherine named for Katherine our mother the apple of father's eyes
(our sister has cautioned me never write about her ever

she has the worst habits of both her parents   dark   mean
as you spoke to one another in separate rooms all through childhood)

across that space where the Cadillac backed into your lane
as you were going for milk with your helmet on   just off the curb

"you were a hidden treasure and loved to be known"
across that space we tell you so

ATTRIBUTES AND ECCENTRICITIES
OF W. WARREN HARPER

his distinct whistle like none other, including the trill,
though he seldom sang out loud his voice pacing and restraint distinctive

he always spoke of his grandfather's deep resonant voice
Plummer Alexander who jumped down from a fence at thirteen

and rode north with Sherman's liberating Army
only to return by Pullman years later, to buy his mother shoes

the story of his tutelage as valet to Huntington Hartford
his learning to read at the Underground Railroad Station

in Ithaca, New York, taught by his wife, the mother of Florence

Alexander that charting to swallow by fine tuning his improvised genealogical
    page

in his I'M KATHERINE memoir
Inventiveness of chores(repeat repeat)to keep you off the streets

and out of trouble USE TROUBLE the title of my next book in press
no doubt influenced by W. Warren Harper as HONORABLE
    AMENDMENTS '95
beforehand

copious knowledge of sports all sports why he became a New
York Giant fan because of John McGraw and what he saw on the Polo
    Grounds

before and after Willie Mays 1950 . . . 1951 year of departure for Coliseum
(wins and losses on the stock market Roland and Alice in '29 crash

in no hurry to get back to Brooklyn to pick up the pieces no record
of Alice visiting her brother Howard in Paris working for Jay Gould

but letters in German of Roland's pursuits in debonair elan opera
"injun joe" Dr. Johnson called haberdashery style 'Warren'

when he appeared at the door of 902 in a green suit "I had a
suit like that once" wwh a perfect 40 regular with no alterations in the best
    stores

as "Lonnie" Chapman said under his breath your father could
wash his car in a suit with a garden hose and not get wet

his meticulous care of his body 'mediation' his taking his time
bailing MSH and JPH out of Rimpau jail over Veterans Day 11 11 '62

a believer in contracts to be signed and fulfilled fair but stern
(one should ask oneself did he or she ever pay back the full amount
    borrowed?)

3rd Neptune Society 'burial at sea' (Jonathan'77/Katherine'88)
not ever a hipshooter as his wife Katti "your loving mother my sweet"

master of crossword the *New York Times* Sunday paper
believer in secrets a correspondence with his beloved no one read

restraint with candor his mantra ask no quarter give no quarter
except within the family never asked for deference from his son at P.O.

Terminal Annex at the workplace
but sacred space at the homestead 2207 do not be late for dinner ever

more than his own children
raised and fed at his table

his memoir a testament to luck of choosing
his lifetime partner 'a feminist' before the word was known or used

"a scrupulous meanness" (James Joyce) with a large sweet tooth
pride in all his kin and therefore a kinsman as mason oddfellow

his limousine ride to the Getty Museum as honored guest
delivered to the podium by Professor Anani Dzidzienyo of Brown faculty

as his personal escort meeting Gwendolyn Brooks ("We Real Cool")
at Ralph Ellison's Memorial on Broadway & 166th

eating pigsfeet on New Year's Eve the fixings by Fanny Ellison
trips to Catskill, Westbury, Cocoa Beach

giving away Christine Webb for Randy Webb fellow CCC W. VA worker
naming "Slim" his German shepherd, after Sterling Brown's tall tale teller

Slim Greer "At One With" tv program on Robert Hayden poet laureate
who had to join the SAG before being paid by NBC local programming

Fred Berwick interviewer classmate from LA State Romantic specialist
driving the trolley ringing the bell on the Toronto Ontario trolley

with Oktay Aksan at the controls a native of Turkey head of his clan
the best seats in the house for "Show Boat" with his sister, Winifred

during the MLA Convention driven door to door by his son
courtesy of Vartan Gregorian president of Brown University (a man of
    influence)

Bowdoin Festival in Brunswick, Maine site where his son was honored
where he had breakfast with Nobel poet and wife Marie at bed & breakfast

with signed copy of Seamus Heaney's THE SPIRIT LEVEL
returning the favor with signed copy of his memoir I'M KATHERINE

dining at high table and copious room service at Hotel Nikko in SF at MLA
holding Roland in SF before he got meningitis

pulling the plug on JPH after ten days on life support told by his wife
listening to Miles and Trane "On Green Dolphin Street" "My Cheri Amour"

"the Secret Life of Plants"   "What's Going On"   "Night Fever"
"Ray Charles" "God Rest Ye Merry Gentlemen" at Xmas by MJQ

Horace Silver and the Jazz Messengers "The Tokyo Blues" Dinah
     Washington
Joe Williams and Count Basic Bags & Trane Duke and Mahalia Jackson

Being Taken Out to Breakfast with Darwin who named him "Buddy"
haircuts at home by Tess for practice and pay

wearing his hat in the garden while watering talking to Ebbie
driving his mustang '65 to jacaranda fragrance   amidst the droppings

my mother talking to the plants birds flowers trees
the photo gallery love of people "in rags outarags and no damned rags at all"

"it's a wise blues that knows its father" Kath from his memoir
his "caretaker supreme" his left handed righthand with her name on his
     checkbook

Freud wrote that the most trying moment in a man's life was the
death of the father ask my sister his daughter what is true?

his love of reading the Raj visiting the UK on Masterpiece Theatre
"the Forsyte Saga" by Galsworthy the paradox "they enslaved us" "straight, no
     chaser"
(theonliest Monk)

Brooklyn College and St. John's law classes the bar   his taking
and passing the most difficult two sections never taking it again

fainting after his wisdom teeth were pulled during '47 blizzard
26" of snow   his hatred of shoveling ("your mother does no floors" at seven)

seeing him regaled in the NY Times Board Room during an annual
Yaddo Meeting Andryanna in Buddy's Brown University cap

ceremonial kente from Anani for Katherine from the town of Bonwire
seat of the Golden Stool heart of the Akan godhead of the Ashanti

from THE PALM WINE DRINKARD by Amos Tutuola "God is So Good"
    to
any vexing problem his son's detention in Soweto '77 asked to write an
    op-ed

in 800 words they wanted to censor Bishop John Albert Johnson's purchase
of freehold land(1908) for a women's dormitory named for JAJ's best friend

Bishop Koppin's wife Fanny seeing JAJ's homestead in Evaton, South Africa
eight miles from Sharpeville where the passbook protestors were shot in the
    back while
running away

Oliver Jackson's mural on the subject his gifts to the family
visionary iconography gracing the homestead from the homeland

MEDITATION ON CATSKILL CREEK

"The snow is about to fall in another fateful blizzard"
    but I am steady at the throttle after visiting North Street

Bushnell Avenue with perennial wet cellar
Koeppel Avenue where you have to post

a relative light enough to pass
to purchase a house near a proper school

still my father had to leave this town
to maneuver the Civilian Conservation Corps

send the largest parcel of groceries to no homestead
he would ever invest in again a pittance for himself

his writing letters for the blacks who received 'care'
packages from the farms of the new confederacy

of which he had his choice being literate Injun Joe
his newfound outsider Canadian father-in-law

would call him   by then he had secured a haberdashery
post from an Irishman with taste saved his money in cans

opened a Christmas fund which my mother fed
at 25 cents a week at year's end she had a check

she could cash show her father my old man
could take care of us while she took care of her mother

who sang only one song "Sometimes I Feel
Like a Motherless Child" to a first born son

who walked early hated his nap
awakening in a rage which my mother obliged

by stepping over a wreathing tantrum
strewn out on the living room floor

He would have no candy it would rot his teeth
keep his little brother in tow as best he could

by unlocking the downstairs outhouse with a pin
he borrowed from his sister's diaper

which he had changed while his mother changed
her mother's the song still new

to the boy who lost his esp even before shul
certainly before catechism Mrs. Silver calling home

to make his father take off a full day
from postal scheme classes at St John's Law

the boy a Giant fan in a Dodger neighborhood
where nothing was ever integrated

for you were Bums the Nits and Jollystompers
emperors of the green at all local parks

until the Navy Street gang
came down with their trucks automatics

when we had pipes and zipguns
or nothing at all from the camphor 'round our necks

my mother our witchdoctor always said
'your hometown was a dump'

your smarts and good looks
an embarrassment

My old man never told her about CCC camp
his driving the forbidden truck for garden truck

for his squadron around Williamsburg
Virginia but never through town(for the whites)

your restoration the flats and beaches
after the blizzard of '47 when Jackie

broke the color line 26" inches of snow
you fainted on the steps while shoveling

your wisdom teeth in your sidepocket
(your mother does no floors you told me

and I took the steps as well)
my esp broken by Japangy Wibecan Kelly thugs

who never served mass took umbrage in the territories
where "Snowball" skipped school

and LeRoy Clark refused to graduate
(master of the flag squad and gymnasium)

Memorial Minutes are in order
to the town and country town

on the New York Thruway entryway
where you get your ticket early and late

dust off the windshield of snowflake and blood
move N or S on Federal byways of the New Deal

which was already over nra(National Relief Act)
the homesteads lost and found

in the memory bank of a kid
taught to read before kindergarten

neither Dutch or German
but still writing letters home

to the frozen belt of a certain whipping
(for my old man said what he did only once)

recruiting what could not be spoken
unless my kinfolk spoke

for the wagon the tools of making a living
when there was no equipment anyone could own

that would guarantee
your paltry wages

where the wages of dying
are unlove: sometimes I feel like a motherless child

as he was
I am

water water everywhere
and not a clear drop to drink

if god is willing and the creek don't rise
I'll be there in springtime father

———

TALK THERAPY ON JOHN MILTON

———

"Paradise Lost" was Rimpau Station
 (the LA River basin no longer dry)

Veterans Day regimen reading in down hours
 collapsing at UCLA Library over Samuel Baugh

Book IV of Milton Paul Zall's assignment
 after metrics in Dryden and Pope *(strategic technical writing)*

variance of Milton's conceit of the couplet lost
 on my 33rd degree Mason inmate *(only cellmate allowed with a hat)*

while my brother was in adjacent cellblock within earshot
 (the paradisal conceit of devil-incarnate *arraignment*)

as I would avoid **"entrainment"** through the offices of Maurice Hartwick
 "young men from Indiana looking for another whorehouse in my backyard"

sound and sense of the local brewery
 (Justice's sonnet on the garden of eden alive in Berryman's

dictum): the fruit of no taste whatsoever the call of eden
 so when I appeared in class to flex each first of three books

(all other inmates being absent): Book IV the devil's arraignment:
praxis still on the buried couplet of Milton's blindness

where touch smell sight full imagery of Ives' mischief
    (while the devil as asp eats dirt before smell gave him scent)

what it is like to be jailed in Pico Station in **1962**
    with a good book to conjugate declensions of power (Vet's Long
    Weekend)

in the great chain of being   stay in the moment
    that of the word treasury of all classics of the journey motif

of goodness and its opposite *"unity in opposition"*
    as only Satan would know it   penultimate to the King of every universe

---

LOVESONG

Millicent Hudson once sent me
a ticket home from Iowa City
I took the train from Marion
sick with cold in freezing rain
that no plane could maneuver
but Cedar Rapids was behind me
when I got off in Oakland
got back on later for LA
(there was a girl working on Lady
at Stanford, her friend "my man")
Stegner in charge; reading Henry James
and taking lsd under control
back and forth to La Honda
I would not speak about the Writers' Workshop
in LA I gave back the unused ticket
Millicent was a poet herself and stacked
a scar across her nose

her laugh a speaking tone of Sassy
incredible to touch
as I recovered from the Hawkeyes
where is she now
who could have translated
any ticket stub I had
in that transgression called manhood
too working class for parents
too tight to ever let me go

1965 WATTS RIOT

I watched this on C.B.S. news from New (Long Lake)
London, Minnesota, 56273 out of Alexandria feed
when I watched at all; *'this will set your people back
one hundred years,'* Lyal said; my answer, from the patio,
armed in L.A. lifeguard shorts, *"they built the country
let them burn it down,"* and race rituals
turned summersaults into race relations,
as I drove off with his daughter
to the bay area, where she would complete school
rather than sell tail in the Fillmore district
of the Group Areas Act, in our *"apartheid"* section:
if you could not feel safe in S.F. where could you feel
safe in America; even at S.F.S.U. there were police, pickets,
and me driving "Sug" to study in the school library
while she waited for 'respiratory-distress-children'
to hatch prematurely, to incubator, *isolette,*
and never her arms to comfort, and not to suckle.

I have no memories of how her relatives "across the bay"

could abandon her, sell baby-furnishings and clothes,
to one they knew as blood; I cannot forget them.

And I cannot forgive you, America, with your obsessions,
disabling even the kindest regard into armed camps
which are not **bantustans**, off-color sweet oases.

And I must address my children who survived,
and who will not ever know their father's
grief at stud poker, the driving wheel
of art and song in graffi-American parlance:

I would sum it up as turkey feathers,
and the value of the birds
in their containers;

                    at Roaring Stoney
where her father sent us on what he imagined
-would be a lovely *honeymoon*,

                               it was deserted;
in town, on all forks of the *Little Crow River,*
we could not live among you;

                    no number of *Uncle Tom's Cabins*
or *Huck* and *Jim* could civilize this terrain,
even on water; you can erase Chippewa names
with every tarbrush and never feel at home:

I must teach this to my children; how to live
across the blood, how to portage, how to transfuse
hate to love; how to disseminate, how to ease;

in *1991* there was another L.A. riot, on my mother's birthday,
though she was already three years gone;

we must traverse the news together, all that's reported,
all on the cutting room floor; and in the heart
of she who walked to school up Holloway Avenue
and should have taken the trolley downtown
to **bart**, and gone across to see her people:

DOMESTIC RELATIONS (DEFENDANT SAITH)

interregnums: **you said too little**
I said too much

Softly as possible through your scream
I offered what the lawyers would get

as *mediation*;
you called me a monster

scylla and charybdis
as portals to chaos

one should not eat the children
who are caught in the web

as to the mast
what is between us

10 children in a letter to grandma
5 on the ocean floor

when I faced down your father
during the **Watts** riot

there was commitment
watermelon eaters

as the outlet
of the Long Lake

where I had been struck
by lightning in an open canoe

eaten chokecherries
without any *sugar*

swum to the point
under the highlines

exposed at sea
in the summer of *1965*

on the **irt** to and from the Bronx
during the drought

where two inches of water
was all you could bathe in

666 was the honeymoon
suite near MoMA

you cried, so hurt in the feet
they thought I'd beaten you

would not let me sit down
in the undertow carriage

THE RED DRESS: 12 24 65

San Francisco

Homemade. The banns woof and warp
of a Minnesotan lutheran minister
reminds the black presence, husband-
to-be, the goodness of "Sleepy Eye"
women, their devotion, the synod
"cathechism of country school"
adrift in fundamentals
which will sustain for a lifetime.

The witness from Guatemala
moves over the vestments of his homemade
chapel as an angel amidst the stigmata,

all the primateurs of Jesus
now descended from the cross,
ascending with the red robe
into the heavens.

As one who does not believe,
and pregnant with his first child,
he wonders what baptism
there will be when zygote
announces to the world
his worldly mission,
how we will guide him
to his compression.

And when he stutters
in kindergarten
how the soft signs
of an E. Coli infection
spun into meningitis
will be but a low hurdle
in the medicine,
phenobarbitol surely,
with no history of side effects

and no guilt to his mother,
who could not nurse him
while he staggered in shots
in his isolette at permanente.

I loved this woman in the red dress,
the vertical and horizontal
access of the quilt she makes
of her inheritance, nails bitten
down, the freezing water
in her bedroom, cycles of bedwetting,
her gnashing teeth,
the colorscheme of dreamscape
as only a fructose

in her bloodlines: sugar
her given nickname

asked what she cannot give
to anyone but first love
and this red wedding dress not his.

WALKING TOUR (LAKE WINDERMERE)
STUDIES IN ROMANTIC POETRY

When the stars threw down their spears,
And watered heaven with their tears,
Did he smile his work to see?
Did he who made the Lamb make thee?
["The Tyger," William Blake]

Just one stitch.
                    The trip to town
is beyond scenic; years from now
you might tell me the dream
so intense you had to be sewn
up, and I have picked you from the floor
in morning sickness, and in attack.

Overpriced on lake district fare,
on poetry, on scenery,
on accents from the continent,
on roads, the childish wonder,
half in step with new meanderings,
anticipating the underground,
dreading the museums.
                    'Go Fish'

in the lake, cover your bait,
prepare for high table at the inn.

It is springtime; you have your book
on English gardening; I am at sea;
three babes want London at any price,
the M4 is waiting, and the M1.

For a small price, on a grant to supplement,
I am nursing single malt over "Romantic" tradition,
sabbatical cost, and a busted lip
which could be gall bladder, such intense pain

but is roe, a dozen apple trees to be pruned,
and all diseased in the dreaded arbor of lost edenic glare
a neighbor and 'friend' about to raise my children
if you will, The Master Sailor of Prudence Island, beware beware.

WALKING TOUR (LAKE WINDERMERE): ITS AFTERMATH

What the hammer? what the chain?
In what furnace was thy brain?
What the anvil? what dread grasp
Dare its deadly terrors clasp?
["The Tyger," William Blake]

Part I

Just one stitch.
            The trip to town
is beyond scenic; years from now
you might tell me the dream
so intense you had to be sewn

up, and I have picked you from the floor
in morning sickness, and in attack, evil gallstones to come.

Overpriced, on poetry, on scenery,
on accents from the continent,
on roads, the children wonder,
half in step with their new positioning,
anticipating the underground,
dreading the museums
                              'Go fish'
in the lake, "cover your bait,"
prepare for high table at the inn of romance, of fantasy.

It is springtime; you have your book
on *English* gardening; I am at sea;
three babes want London undergrounds at any price,
the M4 is waiting, and the M1.

For a small price, on a grant to supplement a terror of prosody,
I am nursing *single* malt over "Romantic" tradition,
sabbatical cost of wayfaring strangers, and a busted lip
which could be gall bladder, such intense pain

be it *roe*, a dozen apple trees to be pruned, thorn in eye:
"Manny Bettencourt" Portuguese sailor about to raise my children
Master of Prudence Island, 'friend' of Mrs. Tompson:
for what is a greenhouse but a hothouse of plenty, pewter-craftsman,
jack of all trades, master of none, but the lonely epicene-cuckold-true.

Part II

Later 'vale of soulmaking' from Keats's LETTERS
And later still "The Squire of Taunton" in deadpan at New Bedford
    courthouse

Melville and Douglass twin celebrants in times of war at homelandstead
And no peace in T. E. Lawrence's motorcade from Isherwood's

"Literature Between the Wars"—their fathers unmentionable—
At Churchill College my "deputy" son, *Patrice Cuchulain Harper*,

introduced his father at campus pub in "**negative capability**" for Arc
Publications, the Rudyard Kipling Pub of grand illusions
then walked 'the Bermuda Triangle' St. Paul's of the ancestors to heaven.

THE SQUIRE OF TAUNTON

---

*[(in U.S.) a justice of the peace, local judge, or other local
dignitary (chiefly used as a title) in country districts and small
towns. (in England) a country gentleman, esp. the chief landed
proprietor in a district.]*

He pulls up into the garage
on twenty acres of land,
a greenhouse in progress,
a pickup truck, '48 Studebaker
green, and no fire of newspaper
to heat up the fuel line,
the down battery,
three kinds on a large lawn,
his daughter halfway up a tall
pine, and once seated buck
naked on a spread with fresh
clothes, perhaps to be run over
by a father in a hurry:
and so he blew his top
at the precise moment,
4 P.M., when he had to be in town,
and swept her up to her bedroom,

and began the punishment,
the lash of his eye on the bedstead,
animal books, pastry, fruit:
when her brother put his thin
chest between them,
head up in the clouds of his natural
uncut hair, and said in a high voice
like a choirboy in penultimate chant
to the bishop, who was drunk on the rite,
"beat me instead of my sister,"

and the song of the bedspread
announced itself as fresh laundry
from Huck's raft, which is where she was
in the circular driveway, unplowed
of clothes and socks, and a few apples
still unswept by the matron,
off on her twenty acres, *plotting*
a cotton field, some corn, okra, greens:

in that instant the squire,
in the service to his woman,
boss of his children, *"fool on a fool's errand,"*
astride the trail to knighthood
in the wrong colony
eighteen miles away,
that squire, infantile in his own district,
with neighbors aligned to *Angola,*
a secret servitude to class, mestizo
cuisine, a fireman with a bad back,
two boys down the road in Sunday
habit, tow Celtic nominals, tow brats,
all ate from the squire's dozen
apple trees, too much unpicked
unsprayed, plantation sweetened Taunton

delicious, this squire, who walked
out I-195 in the '78 blizzard
to see his borrowed house lit up
in exhaust of the plows
became a sentry to peace
in his *anger,*
enforced his love:
sang, silently aloud,
in the snow_____

II

Chaucer, the bard who died in 1400 A.D.
escaping the plague on all the various houses
woke up from dream-allegories from Latin
Italy France when Dante Boccaccio eagles
in vulgate as sails from '*The Black Death*'
the symmetry of women in perpetual garden-truck

this *"bard"* unable to luck or open the perpetual greenhouse
with no "cash crop" the city and the countryside lost angels
of serfdom idiomatic 'manners' courtly pleasures unmanifest
always lost on back roads in the arteries of enemies and strangers
that *muse* was not lost on his jailers who ate from his garden
truck feasted on the bankers and scribes of commerce

'*it is the man outside who judges*' and refuses to kill
those at his table garden truck greenhouse apple orchard
maker of smelt and roe and the snowbird killing the goose
who laid the golden egg and all other "framed tales" into captivity
to wake up in solitary splendor in 'the poet's corner' *elsewhere:*

Note: "The Squire of Taunton" is a trope from Lawrence F. Sykes, photographer and
photocollagist. He and Bernard E. Bruce, Sr. helped MSH move away from this spread of
twenty acres and a four bedroom house, with porch, double-car garage and greenhouse, in
summer, 1978, "the end of innocence" for the poet.

JAXON'S FIRST SONG: 5 21 2000

In the annals of the first song
there is a bridge to "Black & Blue"

as sung by Thomas "Fats" Waller
born on your natal day in 1904

he had symphonic possibilities
somehow curtailed in asinine minstrelsy

Ellison used this motif in Pops's
version of the song in INVISIBLE MAN

you will learn this doubletalk
in two idioms and not be bothered

"bridge" is a musical affinity
to openended possibility

though couched in technical notions
of brand X or X generation

and Ellison's novel has bookends
prologue and epilogue as framed tale

to how to walk that walk
talk that talk

letting the spirit get you over
any bridge(even spontaneous song)

which I hope you sing to yourself
letting others adjust to the pitch

of "Aint Misbehavin'"
Waller's show tune in your honor

NATAL VISIT ON THE THEME OF SHOES

You have called me beforehand
with the good news of the baby turning

acupuncture has done the trick of Chinese
medicine and your doctor approves via sonogram

Your feet are beginning to swell
you have taken off your rings and bracelets

in preparation for what could be a 'c' section
but as I said 'the baby has turned'   perhaps for good

I point out the shoes from land's end with no heel
and pass "discover" to you to order

what used to be called 'the house of the happy feet'
(the Savoy ballroom quipped by Lana Turner

ages and ages ago when 'imitation of life' was vogue)
but this is no film of the American diaspora

and race prevails with gender so you go back to work
with your good news   and unfinished business

your brother about to get on a train after MoMA
(he cannot be Picasso or Matisse but his own man)

we must all teach him to walk the walk
on his own stand   trees   bandstand natchez trace

so we go on in the dance of our lives
never knowing enough for any newborn

who will ask questions of all of us
forgive us for all our sins   those of omission strong

you are already singing to him or her
as you dream night after night of being breathless

so close is she to your heart of hearts
so if at the turning and beyond he comes

in a line of procession of angels
concentrate on omphalos   a string of pearls

ordered from a catalog
in comfortable feet

your beating heart
awaiting the gift of acupuncture

APOLOGIA TO CHARLOTTE SCOTT
ON PANTOPS MOUNTAIN

Our Nathan one day short of his 60th anniversary gone home to await you
(news one never wanted to process: bad news now upon us our prayer shawl)

Under certain stress made reservations to travel on JetBlue from Logan
    airport
(for the last time found my name on 'no fly list'—drove back home to
    Providence)

Rental vehicle from Richmond to Charlottesville no longer applicable
(cancelled local hotel fare near UVA: missed Epiphany mass goodbye without
    calling)

Have not mailed the Fret Cycle nor Use Trouble for you to parse in only your
    handwriting
(program of the ages with friends/family/kin ceremonially lost:
    tears&laughter redux)

Who will stand in your place of Arts&Letters in Cambridge now that you've
    gone away
(custom&ceremony deluxe, extensions of family and colleagues—even
    enemies stunted)

Caduceus in my mother's Bible framed in neighborhood song: who will set
    the table
(news from Chaplin Jewelnel Davis: Charlottes's Barnard service-continuum
    recorded)

Out of such depression comes a chant of saints across our many thresholds
(suffering and grace: fond remembrance of vale of soulmaking epiphanies to
    dwell upon)

And who will set our table: 'bodily decrepitude is wisdom'
radical negative capability our devotionals: 'young we loved each other and
    were ignorant'

FORTY: 6 28 06

You are now under 200 pounds with daily treadmill: stairmaster
(in your teens you hid in geometry room at Mary Wheeler school)

Now the reading clubs of Genes & Gender stifle at the Rock
(as you work your way out of seizure to closure)

What could have been your Nature decodes inward: Powell Assoc's
(I remember E. Coli & **meninges** stricken: tidal messaging now e-mail)

How does one listen from these distances: birthmarks of the genome
(off-pitch the phonemes of stylus are neutered in stammering)

To be caught on **dvd** with babe in arms not your own nor your sister's
(the majesty of caretaking again an idyll of caves)

LOYALTY

for Marge Montgomery

"the self is not a genie in a bottle"
—William Blake

Clean up the leftover cheese,
take it home if you want;
the chiming malevolence of the padre,
adrift in sparkling details of cost.

You were asked to dust the high corners
of the office, and refused;
that got you fired, though it took months,
and now you're involved in investments—
somewhere near the heart of the matter
is a **krugerrand**, closer than *Zimbabwe*.

Ida's ghost comes up in the dream
of your children, all spread out
in colleges, high-tech, the boarding
school that seasons the young,
that seasons meat in the oven,
new furniture in the yard, replaced
silverware that never tarnishes.

Your lights were on the day the **Reverend King**
died, ostracized so near the military
base, nearer to the dropped womb
of Catholic services, parchment sermons.

In the fires that came from within
the cities ignited across **Azania**
while the new eden wore itself out
in the draft, in marches, memorial summits.

This is how you are told goodbye,
take up the cheese that is ordered
in your name, eaten on the run,
let the words be want, poverty
of the pill when light flashes,
chimeras of DNA, the sloegin *pentagon,*
route to the beachfront mansion,
the rocks   the gauntlet below.

Pills and the fear of the truth
break in the lozenges of the spirit,
come back in luncheons
where the black maid
sits down as equal
to shed her tears.

Her *name* doesn't matter; her son
picks up the furniture you will leave—
too reticent and proud for any cheese
that is not spread out on crackers
from the commissary, a little *Uncle Ben's*
rice to go with the missing family name.

Ida rises from the bottle like a *genie*
in rinsed hair; conditioned behind her
her veteran children salute to the black
wall, remember the lilt of your *brogue,*
dust off their brogans: dance again.

PAUL URABE [1938–2003]

We have said WHITE ASHES and Nadame humbly
early in the day (after your birth in San Luis Obispo)

we ate from the hundred pound bag of pearl rice
green tea at bulk rate (long before Von's Dairy Products)

we laughed on Ivy St between Laguna/Octavia
a few blocks from the Opera House none of us could sing the vedas

listening to our tunes on a gay alleyway
with no backyard no speakeasies no parking

we did good time 'at the Blackhawk'
the Jazz Workshop on Bwy in the fog

Miles and Trane apart and together
down the block "City Lights" Lawson's hangout

I read you the poems of Bob Kaufman
when "Howl" was old   15 original copies mimeoed

Lawson was writing about the camps in Arkansas
Fuzzy was in Chicago (maybe knew Hayakawa's hideaway

in the pentacostal church on the south side)
remember when Kay Boyle reviewed my poetry

in the chronicle how many chinatown greasyspoons
did we baptize before the renaissance dim sum

when you could afford it you ate higher on the hog
than was good for you that abalone we took out of season

pickup hoops the Spinnaker to hear Bill Evans drool
pacifica fm   then you moved to management

Severna Park foggy bottom of the swamps
(how you could trek back to valley kin)

when I needed a house you found one on Miramar owned
by a Mexican Amador who did repairs kept the rent down

when I could have bought my own house on 17th St
with twin peaks and two bridges I left town instead

saw you at the pier met your children enjoyed Judy's
laugh at old times(Lawson's first cousin)always about family the brood

out of camp but the camp not fully out of them
I knew about those hard hours you never talked about

I watched you wrap your bad knees as you chamoised
your wheels in the driveway took the fine wine

you'd saved for reunions finally took you to concert
AN AMERICAN REQUIEM at the symphony nearby where neither of us
    were members

as a Buddhist you had better not pick pineapples   as in Hawaiian
sushi will do remnants of the fish market for all the clan to eat

one simple pose of you on your walker the stitches plain
so you could walk with a cane at your sister's 80th in Fresno

I can see you on video Von's in the background your first security check
in the mailbox salt & pepper Boddhitree the fertile fields

arias at Lisle Calaveras chapel
the down pedal of Evans's pavanne lone pacifier

YADDO, MRS. AMES AND BLACK MEN

circa 1966

I worked in the icehouse
and she complained:
late hours, bad for compost,
bad for the muse
one person removed;

he thought: I must get my own Yaddo.

Once he stood in the circle
of pine-topped trees
though he has to go to Skidmore to fire ovens

and probably would not have been invited
back
because of the hours he worked 'round the clock

There is a vantage point
at winter table above the office
that allows for every
conversation

including this one:
archival
pastoral
digital as the schematic softens

for one's face sags
during the day
the muscles relaxing

do you want a morning cast?

much laughter [MSH's Iowa BLUES & LAUGHTER]

for "character" talks back
behind the screen

but this is winter

one cannot be trusted
in the outhouse any time of day

and the icehouse
is always one person removed

keeps itself ready for late hours

more monitoring than usual
for this brand of fly in a late, bad time:

ointment too hot for salve on any wound

"Father and Son" one Sunday, on a smoke break, 1938.

INDEX OF TITLES

MICHAEL HARPER is a University Professor & Professor of English at Brown University, where he has taught since 1970. He is a New York Library Literary Lion, a Phi Beta Kappa scholar, and an American Academy of Arts and Sciences Fellow. His many distinctions include the Robert Hayden Poetry Award from the United Negro College Fund, the Melville-Cane Award, the Black Academy of Arts and Letters Award, and the Robert Frost Medal 2008 for lifetime achievement from the Poetry Society of America. This is his sixteenth book.

ILLINOIS POETRY SERIES
Laurence Lieberman, Editor

History Is Your Own Heartbeat
Michael S. Harper (1971)

The Foreclosure
Richard Emil Braun (1972)

The Scrawny Sonnets and Other Narratives
Robert Bagg (1973)

The Creation Frame
Phyllis Thompson (1973)

To All Appearances: Poems New and Selected
Josephine Miles (1974)

The Black Hawk Songs
Michael Borich (1975)

Nightmare Begins Responsibility
Michael S. Harper (1975)

The Wichita Poems
Michael Van Walleghen (1975)

Images of Kin: New and Selected Poems
Michael S. Harper (1977)

Poems of the Two Worlds
Frederick Morgan (1977)

Cumberland Station
Dave Smith (1977)

Tracking
Virginia R. Terris (1977)

Riversongs
Michael Anania (1978)

On Earth as It Is
Dan Masterson (1978)

Coming to Terms
Josephine Miles (1979)

Death Mother and Other Poems
Frederick Morgan (1979)

Goshawk, Antelope
Dave Smith (1979)

Local Men
James Whitehead (1979)

Searching the Drowned Man
Sydney Lea (1980)

With Akhmatova at the Black Gates
Stephen Berg (1981)

Dream Flights
Dave Smith (1981)

More Trouble with the Obvious
Michael Van Walleghen (1981)

The American Book of the Dead
Jim Barnes (1982)

The Floating Candles
Sydney Lea (1982)

Northbook
Frederick Morgan (1982)

Collected Poems, 1930–83
Josephine Miles (1983; reissue, 1999)

The River Painter
Emily Grosholz (1984)

Healing Song for the Inner Ear
Michael S. Harper (1984)

The Passion of the Right-Angled Man
T. R. Hummer (1984)

Immortal Sofa
Maura Stanton (2008)

National Poetry Series

Eroding Witness
Nathaniel Mackey (1985)
Selected by Michael S. Harper

Palladium
Alice Fulton (1986)
Selected by Mark Strand

Cities in Motion
Sylvia Moss (1987)
Selected by Derek Walcott

The Hand of God and a Few
Bright Flowers
William Olsen (1988)
Selected by David Wagoner

The Great Bird of Love
Paul Zimmer (1989)
Selected by William Stafford

Stubborn
Roland Flint (1990)
Selected by Dave Smith

The Surface
Laura Mullen (1991)
Selected by C. K. Williams

The Dig
Lynn Emanuel (1992)
Selected by Gerald Stern

My Alexandria
Mark Doty (1993)
Selected by Philip Levine

The High Road to Taos
Martin Edmunds (1994)
Selected by Donald Hall

Use Trouble
Michael S. Harper (2009)

Theater of Animals
Samn Stockwell (1995)
Selected by Louise Glück

The Broken World
Marcus Cafagña (1996)
Selected by Yusef Komunyakaa

Nine Skies
A. V. Christie (1997)
Selected by Sandra McPherson

Lost Wax
Heather Ramsdell (1998)
Selected by James Tate

So Often the Pitcher Goes to Water
until It Breaks
Rigoberto González (1999)
Selected by Ai

Renunciation
Corey Marks (2000)
Selected by Philip Levine

Manderley
Rebecca Wolff (2001)
Selected by Robert Pinsky

Theory of Devolution
David Groff (2002)
Selected by Mark Doty

Rhythm and Booze
Julie Kane (2003)
Selected by Maxine Kumin

Shiva's Drum
Stephen Cramer (2004)
Selected by Grace Schulman

The Welcome
David Friedman (2005)
Selected by Stephen Dunn

Michelangelo's Seizure
Steve Gehrke (2006)
Selected by T. R. Hummer

Veil and Burn
Laurie Clements Lambeth (2007)
Selected by Maxine Kumin

Spring
Oni Buchanan (2008)
Selected by Mark Doty

Other Poetry Volumes

Local Men and *Domains*
James Whitehead (1987)

Her Soul beneath the Bone: Women's
Poetry on Breast Cancer
Edited by Leatrice Lifshitz (1988)

Days from a Dream Almanac
Dennis Tedlock (1990)

Working Classics: Poems on Industrial
Life
*Edited by Peter Oresick and Nicholas
Coles* (1990)

Hummers, Knucklers, and Slow
Curves: Contemporary Baseball Poems
Edited by Don Johnson (1991)

The Double Reckoning of Christopher
Columbus
Barbara Helfgott Hyett (1992)

Selected Poems
Jean Garrigue (1992)

New and Selected Poems, 1962–92
Laurence Lieberman (1993)

The Dig and *Hotel Fiesta*
Lynn Emanuel (1994)

For a Living: The Poetry of Work
*Edited by Nicholas Coles and Peter
Oresick* (1995)

The Tracks We Leave: Poems on En-
dangered Wildlife of North America
Barbara Helfgott Hyett (1996)

Peasants Wake for Fellini's *Casanova*
and Other Poems
*Andrea Zanzotto; edited and translated
by John P. Welle and Ruth Feldman;
drawings by Federico Fellini and Augusto
Murer* (1997)

Moon in a Mason Jar and *What My
Father Believed*
Robert Wrigley (1997)

The Wild Card: Selected Poems, Early
and Late
*Karl Shapiro; edited by Stanley Kunitz
and David Ignatow* (1998)

Turtle, Swan and *Bethlehem in Broad
Daylight*
Mark Doty (2000)

Illinois Voices: An Anthology of Twen-
tieth-Century Poetry
Edited by Kevin Stein and G. E. Murray
(2001)

On a Wing of the Sun
Jim Barnes (3-volume reissue, 2001)

Poems
*William Carlos Williams; introduction
by Virginia M. Wright-Peterson* (2002)

The University of Illinois Press
is a founding member of the
Association of American University Presses.

———————————————————————

Composed in 10.5/14 Adobe Garamond
with Meta display
by Celia Shapland
at the University of Illinois Press
Designed by Kelly Gray
Manufactured by Cushing-Malloy, Inc.

University of Illinois Press
1325 South Oak Street
Champaign, IL 61820-6903
www.press.uillinois.edu